The Road Home

The Road Home

Images for the Spiritual Journey

Sara Covin Juengst

Westminster John Knox Press
LOUISVILLE • LONDON

Scripture quotations, unless otherwise indicated, are from the New Revised Standard Version of the Bible, copyright © 1989 by the Division of Christian Education of the National Council of the Churches of Christ in the U.S.A., and are used by permission. Scripture quotations marked NEB are taken from *The New English Bible,* © The Delegates of the Oxford University Press and The Syndics of the Cambridge University Press, 1961, 1970. Used by permission. Scripture quotations marked RSV are from the Revised Standard Version of the Bible, copyright 1946, 1952, 1971, 1973 by the Division of Christian Education of the National Council of the Churches of Christ in the U.S.A., and are used by permission. Scripture quotations marked TEV are from the *Good News Bible—Old Testament.* Copyright © American Bible Society 1966, 1971, 1976.

Grateful acknowledgment is made for permission to reprint the following copyrighted material:

Excerpt from "Flight" by Sara Covin Juengst in *Images: Women in Transition,* ed. by Janice Grana, © 1976, p. 134.

Excerpt from "The Rising," *Celtic Prayers, A Book of Celtic Devotion, Daily Prayers and Blessings,* by Robert Van de Weyer, p. 25.

Excerpt from *Psalms of Lament.* © 1995 Ann Weems. Used by permission of Westminster John Knox Press.

Cover design by Pam Poll Graphic Design
Cover art © Fiona Frank/Allsport/Getty Images

First edition
Published by Westminster John Knox Press
Louisville, Kentucky

This book is printed on acid-free paper that meets the American National Standards Institute Z39.48 standard. ∞

PRINTED IN THE UNITED STATES OF AMERICA

02 03 04 05 06 07 08 09 10 11 — 10 9 8 7 6 5 4 3 2

Library of Congress Cataloging-in-Publication Data is on file at the Library of Congress, Washington, D.C.

ISBN 0-664-22426-1

*To the Congregation of the Lincolnton Presbyterian Church,
Lincolnton, Georgia, who have provided me with encouragement,
nourishment, and strength for the journey*

The journey of a thousand miles begins with a single step.
—Lao-tzu (sixth century B.C.)

CONTENTS

PREFACE

My husband and I have moved thirty-one times in our forty-eight years of marriage. We never intended to have such a peripatetic lifestyle. It just happened. We moved across the ocean. We moved just down the street. Once, on a half-hour's notice, we embarked on an eleven-day, ten-country evacuation from the heart of Africa. We moved with one child, with two, with three, and with four. Sometimes we were eager to start down a new road; sometimes we dreaded it. We have traveled autobahns in Germany and have been mired down on muddy dirt roads in the Congo. We have cautiously maneuvered around hairpin turns crossing the Alps and have delighted in the deep South's winding country roads overhung with thick green. We have sped along the endless straightness of the roads that cross midwestern prairies, and have battled the taxis on New York City streets.

Perhaps it is this personal history of journeying that made me want to explore biblical images of roads and journeys. In this book, I have tried to reflect on these questions: Why do people leave the security of home for the risks of the road? How does travel shape and change lives? What help is there for those who travel lonely roads? How does one make wise decisions at important crossroads? Why are the words "way," "path," "walk," and "journey" so integral to biblical spirituality? What is "the heart's true home"? All these questions will be illuminated by reflection on stories of biblical journeys and Scripture passages that serve as lamps to our feet and light to our path as we journey onward.

I am grateful to all those persons who have guided my own faith journey through the years, but would like to acknowledge four of them whose wisdom provided special guidance at crucial times in my life's journey: Charles Arrington, Rachel Henderlite, C. D. Weaver, and Ben Kline. They were all thoughtful guides who pointed me in the right direction.

My special gratitude goes to the women at the Rock Eagle Presbyterian Women's Conference and the Mo-Ranch Women's Conference, who heard some of the ideas in this book in their preliminary stages and encouraged me to put them into print. I am also grateful to the congregation of Lincolnton Presbyterian Church in Lincolnton, Georgia, who have patiently listened to parts of this work in the form of sermons, and whose affirmation provides me with ongoing encouragement and support.

I cannot adequately express my thanks to my editor, Stephanie Egnotovich, who combined competence and kindness to help me produce a more polished work. Her help has been invaluable to me.

I am deeply grateful to my companion of the road for nearly fifty years, my husband, Dan, and to our four children, Eric, Stuart, Adele, and Dan, who traveled with us as we crossed oceans, climbed mountains, roamed through African villages, and searched for home. This book could not have been written without them, and, in a very deep way, it is for them.

Willington, S. C., 2001

1   ROADS IN BIBLICAL TIMES

Set up road markers for yourself,
   make yourself guideposts;
consider well the highway,
   the road by which you went.
              —Jeremiah 31:21

Roads have played an important role in human history from the earliest of times. They were created out of the trackless wilderness because of prosaic needs and strong desires: the need to find good agricultural or hunting locations and good water supplies; the need to escape threats or enemies; the need for barter and trade; the desire for human companionship and social interactions; the desire to explore new places; and the timeless desire for a better way to live. In the twenty-first century, these reasons are still the driving force behind the vast network of superhighways, city streets, and winding country roads that crisscross our planet.

In the introduction to his excellent book *The Roads and Highways of Ancient Israel*, David Dorsey describes the profound influence roads have on a nation's development and history: "Highways determine a nation's demographic patterns to a large degree since population centers generally grow up along communication routes. The positions of roads also dictate or at least prescribe the movement of armies, merchants, and ordinary citizens."[1] Dorsey also suggests that the history of a country cannot be properly understood without a basic knowledge of its geopolitical configuration, including its road system.

I agree with Dorsey, and believe that in order to understand what lies behind ancient biblical stories and grasp the significance of the road metaphors used throughout Scripture, we will benefit from a clearer picture of the role played by road systems in ancient times. The roads that crossed Palestine led to many countries. The most important trade routes in biblical times passed from the Fertile Crescent through Palestine to Egypt, connecting with spice routes bearing caravans from Arabia, India, and the East. Palestine's strategic position astride the vital international roads that linked Africa with Asia meant that the surrounding nations were constantly fighting for its possession. Ancient armies from Egypt, Assyria, Babylonia, Persia, and Rome surged along those Palestinian highways in bloody struggles for domination. Even today, political clashes over domination continue to bloody the streets and highways of that ancient land. As I am writing this, a suicide bomber from a terrorist group has just exploded a bomb on a busy street in the heart of Jerusalem.

TRAVEL IN ANCIENT ISRAEL

For those of us who live in countries laced by paved highways and railroads and spanned by invisible airways, travel is part of the routine of our lives. Few people live without means of transportation, either private or public. We no longer have to depend on our feet to take us where we want to go. Travel was difficult in biblical times. Consequently, in the Old Testament period ordinary people left their homes only rarely. The most likely travelers were people of high social standing, and they were traveling for one of three main reasons: religious requirements; commercial transactions; and political or diplomatic missions.[2]

Travel in response to religious requirements included trips to religious festivals, to feasts, and to cultic centers such as Shiloh, Dan, Bethel, and, of course,

Jerusalem. Three annual pilgrim festivals for which people traveled to Jerusalem were Passover, Weeks, and Sukkot.

Travel for commerce and trade brought international caravans to the major roads and highways of Israel, carrying precious ores from Arabia, cedar from Lebanon, linen from Egypt, spices and gems from Ethiopia. Trade within Israel was largely limited to agricultural products such as wheat, barley, olives and olive oil, wine, and various fruits and vegetables.

Scripture records many instances of travel undertaken for political and diplomatic purposes: trips by royal messengers to keep the king's military commanders informed of the king's wishes, and by court officials, bustling to and fro with edicts and commands, treaties and negotiations, collecting taxes, serving as ambassadors, and visiting potential allies in service of the king. Roads were also necessary for the movement of armies, which, particularly under David's reign, seem to have been constantly on the march.

In addition to these three primary purposes for travel, however, the Bible records an interesting variety of personal reasons that caused more ordinary folk to set out on journeys, among them :

> *Courting a woman.* Samson went down the road called "Way of Beth-shemesh" from his home at Mahaneh-dan in the foothills southwest of Jerusalem to Timnah (probably four miles north of Beth-shemesh) to court a nameless Philistine woman (Judg. 14:5–7).

> *Attending weddings and funerals.* Samson returned along the Way of Beth-shemesh to marry the woman of Timnah (Judg. 14:8–10). Jacob journeyed from Shechem down the central mountain road and was reunited with his father, Isaac, at Hebron (Mamre) after a twenty-year separation. He and Esau buried Isaac there (Gen. 35:28).

> *Looking for a job.* A young man from Bethlehem took the road from his home to seek work as a priest about twenty miles to the north in the hill country of Ephraim near Bethel (Judg. 17:7–12).

Attending a banquet. Absalom invited all his brothers to a sheepshearing festival at Baal-hazor, fifteen miles north of Jerusalem (as a part of his plan for revenge on Amnon for the rape of Tamar) (2 Sam. 13:23–33).

Bringing food home. The "capable wife" brings food "from far away" (Prov. 31:10, 14).

MODES OF TRAVEL

Most traveling was done on foot. This was not always pleasant, for the roads were rough and uneven, and were slippery in rain. They often ran along precipitous cliffs or wound through dry creek beds that were strewn with stones. Sandals did not afford much protection. The hazards of traveling by foot over such treacherous, rocky roads underlie passages in the psalms that praise the God who "made my way safe . . . made my feet like the feet of a deer, and set me secure on the heights" (Ps. 18:32, 33), or ask for protection from enemies "who boast against me when my foot slips" (Ps. 38:16). One of the most beautiful ascriptions of praise in Scripture is in Psalm 56:

> For you have delivered my soul from death,
>   and my feet from falling,
> so that I may walk before God
>   in the light of life.
>
> (Ps. 56:13)

When means of conveyance were needed to carry both people and goods, most people relied on donkeys. Donkeys had been domesticated centuries before Abraham's time in Mesopotamia and Egypt, and even the very poor owned at least one donkey. One indication of wealth was the possession of great numbers of them.[3] Donkeys could cover about sixty miles a day. Many stories in the Bible describe how they were used to carry heavy burdens. In the story of Joseph's brothers' visit to Egypt, they loaded their donkeys with the grain they were taking home to their father Jacob (Gen. 42:26).

Donkeys were also used to carry people. One such account is the humorous folk story of Balaam's talking donkey in Numbers 22:15–35. In Zechariah, the messianic king is pictured as arriving on a donkey rather than a horse, to show that he was coming in peace, not as a warrior. According to Matthew, Jesus was acting out this prophecy when he chose to ride into Jerusalem on a donkey. The accounts of this event are the only places in the New Testament where donkeys are specifically mentioned, except in 2 Peter 2:16, which refers to the Balaam story. It is only an assumption that Mary came to Bethlehem on the back of a donkey, that there was a donkey in the stable, and that the Holy Family left for Egypt on donkey back. It is very likely that the "animal" on which the Good Samaritan placed the wounded man was a donkey, but Scripture does not tell us that.

Horses were not among the animals in the stables of the early Hebrew patriarchs, but they were already in use in Egypt during Joseph's day. Joseph was honored by riding in the chariot of Pharaoh's second-in-command (Gen. 41:43). Nearly all references to horse or mule riding are in military settings. Pharaoh used horse-drawn chariots to pursue the Israelites during the exodus. Although there is a reference to the Canaanite nations' coming out "with very many horses and chariots" to fight against Israel under Joshua's leadership (Josh. 11:4), there are few other mentions of horses in the Old Testament before the monarchy. Perhaps this is because, as one scholar suggests, horses were seen by Israel as "a symbol of pagan luxury and dependence on physical power for defense."[4]

Chariots were used for transporting royalty in peacetime as well as in war. Absalom's vanity was demonstrated by his riding in a horse-drawn chariot preceded by fifty young men (2 Sam. 15:1). Naaman traveled from Syria with horses and chariots to visit Elisha (2 Kgs. 5:9). Chariots traveled even into the hill country, which indicates that there must have been a network of roads wide enough for chariots during Old Testament times. The average road was probably two lanes wide, or three to four yards, and many roads were too narrow for chariots and permitted travel only by foot or animal back. The arrival of chariots may have been responsible for the beginnings of actual road construction, to improve those obstructed by boulders and stones and overgrown with reeds.[5]

Although we associate camels with Bible stories, they were never popular with the ancient Hebrews, and were in limited use until the sixteenth century B.C.[6] They were mentioned in the Old Testament as symbols of the wealth of Abraham, Jacob, and Job. Their use was mostly for traveling or transporting goods across the deserts, and occasionally for carrying supplies in war. They could cover from sixty to seventy-five miles per day.

Aside from figures of speech, the New Testament contains only two references to camels, both of which describe John the Baptist's clothing (Matt. 3:4; Mark 1:6). We are familiar, of course, with Jesus' use of the camel as a hyperbolic metaphor. To describe, for instance, how the Pharisees substitute an emphasis on tithing for the truly important matters of justice, mercy, and faith, he says they "strain out a gnat but swallow a camel" (Matt. 23:24). The Gospels of Matthew, Mark, and Luke record Jesus' proverb about the camel and the eye of a needle (Matt. 19:24, Mark 10:25, Luke 18:25).

WHAT WERE ROADS LIKE IN BIBLICAL TIMES?

Were the roads paved in Old Testament times? Although scholars disagree about this, there is a strong possibility that they were, for Mesopotamian streets from the Old Testament period have been discovered that are similar to later, Roman-built roads. The Hebrew word *mesilla*, usually translated "highway," may actually mean "built up of stone or gravel."

In New Testament times, the Romans, of course, were famous for their roads. They realized the importance of land highways for military and commercial purposes. The Romans' policy of building and maintaining good roads in every new area as the empire expanded helped them maintain peace in the empire. Travel on these roads was generally safe. Inns for travelers were frequent, although early Christians usually depended on the hospitality of other church members. An example of this is the hospitality offered to Paul and his friends by Mnason of Cyprus, referred to as "an early disciple" (Acts 21:16). The Letter to the Hebrews reminded the early Christians that hospitality is to be extended to strangers as well: "Do not neglect to show hospitality to strangers" (Heb. 13:2).

Because no major bridges existed across the Jordan or larger rivers during the Old Testament period, river crossings were made primarily by fording. Ferries, which were common in other countries, are not mentioned in Scripture. Fords, shallow places which permitted easy crossing of rivers and streams, played an important geographical role, determining the location of cities and the routes of major roads.

Roads and cities also had a symbiotic relationship. Cities sprang up along major roads, and roads were constructed to connect one city with others. Roads did not often go through cities in Old Testament times, because cities were walled, usually had only one gate, and were located on the top of a hill or "tel" for protection. Instead, narrow access roads led from the highways to the cities.

Most roads were named according to their destinations, for example, "the Beth-shemesh Road," "the Wilderness Road," or the "Jordan River Road." There's even an Ophrah Road, named for its destination (see 1 Sam. 13:17 KJV). The "Way of the Sea," which led along the coast, actually meant "the road that leads to the sea."

WELL-KNOWN ROADS IN BIBLICAL TIMES

The broken landscape of Palestine was a natural limitation to the travel of the ancient Israelites. Four major routes were used for north-south travel: along the Mediterranean coastal plain, along the crest of the hill country, along the Jordan rift, and on the Transjordan plateau. These north-south routes were linked to east-west roads of local importance. Powerful walled cities, located at intersections of the north-south and east-west roads, owed their wealth not only to the fertility of the surrounding fields, but also to these trade routes. These city strongholds included Megiddo, located at a strategic site on the coastal route, and Shechem, forty miles north of Jerusalem on the hill road.

The most significant of these ancient routes were the north-south roads, which not only connected major cities, but linked Egypt with the Fertile Crescent. These four were known by a variety of names.

The Coastal Route, or the Via Maris

The most important thoroughfare in ancient Israel was undoubtedly the great international coastal highway which ran along the Mediterranean Sea and linked Mesopotamia and Egypt. This highway, called the Via Maris (the Way of the Sea), or the Great Trunk Route, was mentioned by Isaiah, who said, "in the latter time he will make glorious the way of the sea" (Isa. 9:1). The highway was intersected by a network of east-west roads. The location of seaports, such as Joppa on the Mediterranean, played a major role in developing this network.

Mountain passes also played an important role in determining the routes these ancient roads took. The Via Maris followed the Mediterranean coastal plain from Gaza to Aphek, then turned inland through a pass at Megiddo. This pass, the cause and site of many fierce battles, is known by the familiar name of Armageddon. The highway continued across the Plain of Esdraelon, passed between Mount Tabor and the Nazareth hills, brushed the northwest shore of the Sea of Galilee, and crossed the Jordan to Damascus. The Via Maris was the main road to and from Egypt. Ordinary travelers, caravans, diplomats, and armies used it, and it received and carried traffic from Africa to Asia. Many towns and cities were located directly along the Via Maris, and its influence on the history and historical geography of early Israel was profound.[7]

When Joseph's brothers sold him to the Ishmaelite traders, he was taken from Dothan down the Via Maris to Egypt. Later, the route was controlled by the Philistines by means of three fortified cities: Gaza (where Samson pulled down the temple), Ashkelon, and Ashdod. They were eventually subdued by David, and control of this route greatly contributed to David's wealth, and also to Solomon's.

The network of roads along this coastal plain extended to all parts of the land. Such a network bears witness to the importance of Palestine as an important crossroads in biblical times, but also to the frequency of commercial, military, and diplomatic travel along these roads, even if ordinary folk left home only rarely.

The Hill Road: The National Highway

This road ran down the middle of Judea and Samaria. It is referred to by various names: the Hill Road, the Ridge Route, the Way of the Patriarchs, and the Water-parting Route. It followed the crest of the hill country from Beersheba through Hebron, Bethlehem, Jerusalem, Ramah, Bethel, and Shechem to the Plain of Esdraelon. This was the usual route travelers took between Galilee and Jerusalem for festivals, a three- to five-day trip of about seventy-five miles. Today a modern paved highway follows this route closely. Just before the time of Jesus, when the conflict between Jews and Samaritans developed into open hostility, many Jews preferred to take a more circuitous route through Transjordan, to avoid Samaria. This may well be the reason why Jesus, on his last trip to Jerusalem, did not take this road, but, according to Matthew, on leaving Galilee went to "the region of Judea beyond the Jordan" through Perea (Matt. 19:1).

The Jordan Rift or Valley Road

The Valley Road ran along the Jordan valley from Jericho to Scythopolis and then northward to link with settlements on the western shore of the Sea of Galilee. Just as the positions of the seaports along the coast determined the location of the east-west highways connecting with the Via Maris, on the eastern side their location was determined by the fords of the Jordan. At only three places along this highway were there convenient ways to cross the Jordan River. About fifteen miles south of the Sea of Galilee the great fortress of Beth-shan guarded a crossing and the entrance to Jezreel. A second crossing was at the Wadi Farah, where the River Jabbok provided access to the Transjordan heights. It was at this ford that Jacob had his wrestling encounter with God. The third, and most famous, crossing was through the fords just north of the Dead Sea at Jericho. Through these fords ran at least six east-west routes.

The King's Highway: Across the Transjordanian Plateau

The King's Highway, the Transjordanian route, ran along the fringe of the Syrian desert the length of east Palestine, from Damascus in the north to Elath in the south, connecting with roads that led across the Negeb desert toward the coastal route to Egypt. These east-west roads probably joined the spice routes from Arabia, allowing goods from Arabia to be brought into Palestine. The King's Highway is quite likely the route Jacob followed to Haran after his ladder dream at Bethel, crossing the Jordan at the Ford of Jabbok to reach the Highway and continuing north. It is mentioned in Numbers when the Israelites requested permission of the kings of Edom and the Amorites to pass through their lands along this route (Num. 20:17; 21:21–22). When Solomon's empire was at its height, his control of both the Coastal Highway and the King's Highway meant that he controlled trade between Asia and Africa as well as the spice trade from Arabia. He became rich acting as a middleman between the kingdoms of Asia Minor and Egypt. There is little doubt that the journey of the Queen of Sheba (present-day Yemen) to Jerusalem was prompted by commercial considerations.

ROAD TERMINOLOGY

In the Old Testament a number of Hebrew words are translated as "road." The most common is *derek,* which occurs seven hundred and six times in the Old Testament and is found in fifty-nine of the sixty-six books of the Old Testament. It has a broad range of meanings, including stretch of road, journey, style, custom or conduct, God's standards or the behavior required by God, a condition or situation, strength or might. It is also translated as "way" (especially in the KJV), "route," or "highway."[8]

These varied meanings can be summarized under three main ideas: road, journey, or course of travel.

> *Road* includes any kind of thoroughfare: paved highways, footpaths, public roads and private ones, primary roads and secondary ones. It can also be used in a metaphorical way.
>
> *Journey* focuses on the travel itself, as in "They went on their way to go back to the land of Judah" (Ruth 1:7).

Course of travel refers to the pattern of travel, which might be a literal pattern, a behavioral pattern, a moral pattern, or a daily-life pattern as in Psalm 37:5: "Commit your way [*derek*] to the LORD; trust in him, and he will act." Most of the uses of *derek* in the Old Testament include this meaning.

The second most common word is *orah,* which is a poetic synonym for *derek* and has almost the same meanings. It is never used in prose, but only in poetry. *Derek* and *orah* are often used in parallel, as in Proverbs 2:20: "Walk in the way of the good, and keep to the paths of the just." The fact that *orah* appears only in poetry may mean that it was not used in daily speech.[9] The word *natib* also appears exclusively in poetry, and is often translated as "path." *Natib* is never used in the sense of pattern and only rarely as a journey.

There are a number of other words for roads in the Old Testament, each with a slightly different shade of meaning. *Mesilla* is usually translated "highway." It always designates an actual physical road that is a major public thoroughfare, a prepared or constructed road. The word *magal* designates a course of travel that is correctly aligned or straight, not a physical road. *Sebil* is used for a road, a track, or a path. *Misal,* an unusual word for road, is used only once in the Old Testament, in the story of Balaam. *Misal* indicates a path, perhaps with walls on either side, so narrow that one person might prevent the passage of another.

The word *hus* designates a city street, as in Jeremiah 37:21, which speaks of the "baker's street." Streets, in biblical times as today, were the location for public meetings, public preaching (the prophets, Jesus), and public occasions of honor. In Scripture, to describe what goes on "in the streets" is to describe what is going on in the city as a whole.

The street can be a place of anguish. For example, "In all the squares there shall be wailing; / and in all the streets they shall say, 'Alas! alas!'" (Amos 5:16). It can also be a place of joy, as in Zechariah's peaceful picture of the messianic era:

> Old men and old women shall again sit in the streets of Jerusalem, each with staff in hand because of their great age. And the streets of the city shall be full of boys and girls playing in its streets.

(Zech. 8:4–5)

Streets are not, however, generally described as wholesome places, but rather as settings for prostitutes (Prov. 7:12) and the destitute (Lam. 4:5). They are filled with refuse, even with dead bodies (Isa. 5:25). They are muddy, dirty, and forsaken. This makes Jesus' banquet invitation even more striking, because in it he implied that even the disreputable "people of the street" may enter the kingdom.

CONCLUSION

The Bible is a vibrant, exciting drama of life, and much of that drama unfolded along the highways and roads of ancient Palestine. The significance of those routes determined the rise and fall of cities, countries, and their rulers. One cannot fully understand the movements of biblical characters such as Abraham, Joseph, Joshua, Isaiah, Jesus, and Paul without some knowledge of the routes they followed in their journeys. Geography affects a people's history, culture, sociology, and religious practice. The question, Where do we go to worship? is as essential as, Where do we go to buy food? The paths we choose when we come to crossroads, both physical and metaphorical, are crucial to who we are and what we will become. For those of us who have chosen to be "followers of the Way," it is important to understand the kind of roads and ways that are set forth in Scripture.

2   THE JOURNEY BEGINS

Leaving Home

He set out, not knowing where he was going.
　　　　　　　　　—Hebrews 11:8

Afoot and light-hearted, I take to the open road,
Healthy, free, the world before me.
　　　　　　　　　—Walt Whitman

O to be out on the road
and going one knows not whither nor where.
　　　　　　　　　—Vachel Lindsay

The road goes ever on and on
Down from the door where it began . . .
　　　　　　　　　—J. R. R. Tolkien

Taking to the road assumes leaving home. Every journey implies leaving behind—metaphorically or literally—that which is known and familiar, even if that leaving behind is a healthy move from the best possible of motives.

Scripture is full of stories of people leaving home: Abraham and Sarah, Joseph, Jacob and his family, the exodus, the exile to Babylon and the return, Joseph and Mary with their infant son, Jesus leaving Galilee for Jerusalem, the prodigal son,

Paul, and a host of others. These stories are the stories of our own lives as well. They resonate with and call forth our own experiences of excitement, discovery, apprehension, and anticipation as we leave the familiar for the open road.

In 1956, my husband Dan and I said good-bye to life as it had always been and went to live in the Belgian Congo, a country we had never seen. We left our homes, our families, and the security of the known to live on another continent among people who spoke a different language and had different customs of food, dress, and worship. It was not easy. Both of our fathers died while we were overseas, and in those days before e-mail we did not learn of their deaths until weeks later. We missed our families and friends. I frequently dreamed of the luxury of going to a Woolworth's five-and-dime to buy such unattainables as crayons and safety pins. The move was a drastic change in our lifestyles, our expectations, and our values.

Dan and I discovered that leaving home or starting down a new road can be many things: a joyful adventure, a time of self-discovery, a painful break, a scary risk, or even an act of rebellion. Our going to Congo incorporated all of these in varying degrees.

LEAVING HOME AS A JOYFUL ADVENTURE

In the mid-1940s, after wartime gas rationing was lifted, my father's favorite Sunday afternoon family activity was a leisurely drive in our Oldsmobile. "Let's go for a ride!" he would say with a joyous lilt in his voice. We all dutifully piled in the car, my three siblings and I arguing over who would sit next to the windows, and sneaking books along to read when the scenery got boring. The lure of the road had not gotten to us yet. It was my father's particular delight to explore the narrow, winding back roads of the Carolina countryside. "Let's see where this one goes!" he would murmur, and Mother would sigh with apprehension. There were a lot of dirt roads in South Carolina in the '30s and '40s, or, to be more exact, there were a lot of red clay roads that were treacherous after a rain. As the car slipped and slid while negotiating those clay slopes, we children were thrilled, and loved to shout out,

"Ooshy-gooshy, ooshy-gooshy!" while my mother murmured nervously, "Be careful, John!" Over time, my father's excitement infected me as well, and today I can never pass a small country road that meanders through woods and over hills without wanting to "see where it goes."

The lure of the open road has been a favorite theme of poets for centuries. The road beckons to the adventure and excitement that are just around the corner or over the horizon. Walt Whitman wrote about that sense of freedom and discovery, of "the world before me." Wanderlust is powerful. Horizons have a powerful pull: the tantalizing blue sweep of mountain ranges or the distant rim of the ocean tug at us, saying, "Come, see what I have to offer!"

Dan and I could not wait to get to the Congo in 1959. I still remember the rush of excitement I felt as our plane approached the capital city of Leopoldville. Looking down, we saw an African village spread along a road, with the mud-walled, thatched-roof homes I had pictured in my mind for so long. The joyful adventure was beginning. The dirt road unwinding below us was a symbol of our journey into a new life.

Although we tend to associate this yearning for adventure with youth and the beginning of independence, it is more and more a pattern for people of all ages. Travel is often cited as one of the goals of retirement. Senior citizens like going to places they have never visited and having experiences previously unimagined: watching voodoo ceremonies in Haiti, doing the shag at Myrtle Beach, South Carolina, or building a Habitat house in Mexico.

In J. R. R. Tolkien's classic fantasy *The Lord of the Rings,* one of the characters sings "The Old Walking Song"—which speaks of following an almost never-ending road that joins other roads and moves in new directions. A brief quote is at the chapter's beginning. This ballad became our family theme song because of our many moves, and because of the way it describes the mingled anticipation and apprehension we felt in those moves.[1]

Abraham and Sarah

I like to think that Abraham and Sarah set out from Haran with the same spirit of joyful adventure as Dan and I felt. The words in Hebrews 11 seem so optimistic:

"By faith Abraham obeyed" . . . "he was called" . . . "an inheritance"; . . . "he set out, not knowing where he was going." The Genesis story carries the same tone of eager obedience: "So Abram went." Norman K. Gottwald speaks of the "sense of restlessness and inner urging" accompanying the "divine directives and promises" that characterizes the sagas of the patriarchs.[2]

Abraham and Sarah—late in life—left life as it had always been and ventured into the unknown. They had no way of knowing what lay before them, but they surely knew things would never be the same for them. Author Robert Raines describes their leaving in this way: "Something inside them would not be denied, could not be ignored, had to be honored, no matter who understood or didn't."[3] Abraham was "called" out to the road, and Scripture testifies that he was faithful to that call.

The Apostle Paul

In the New Testament, there is no clearer picture of joyful adventure than in the stories of Paul's missionary journeys. The resurrection had given new energy to the scattered followers of Jesus. From the moment they heard the news, they set out to proclaim what God had done. No other faith has ever spread so far so fast. Paul was not the only Christian missionary, nor was he always successful, but he was zealous, and eager, and joyful. Luke tells us that even when he and Barnabas met with a hostile reception from the Jews of Pisidian Antioch, they were "filled with joy and with the Holy Spirit" (Acts 13:52) because of the positive response of the Gentiles who heard their words with gladness.

Without question, Paul knew himself called to be "a light to the Gentiles," which meant leaving home for the joyful adventure of bringing God's salvation "to the ends of the world." It was with the assurance of his divine commission that he embarked on his journey to central Asia Minor, to the Aegean world, to Illyricum, and then on to Rome and (in intention at least) to Spain. His conviction that he was God's chosen instrument to bring Gentiles to faith gave wings to his feet, and filled him with dynamic energy. The road that lured him covered thousands of miles, and along it he endured frightful abuse: "afflictions, hardships, calamities, beatings, imprisonments, riots, labors, sleepless nights, hunger" (2 Cor. 6:4–5).

Amazingly, in spite of all that, he could declare "We do not lose heart" (2 Cor. 4:1). Why did he do such a curious thing? He did it because, like Abraham and Sarah, something inside "would not be denied, could not be ignored, had to be honored."

Our Call to Joyful Adventure

The call of God summons us from easy chairs onto winding roads, rocky paths, and thorny ways. It puts into our minds a hope for new vistas, a craving for new understandings, a thirst for living life on a different plane of discipline and discovery, and a "holy discomfort" with ourselves. As one minister expressed it, "God's call puts wheels on my feet." As in Abraham and Sarah's case, answering that call means leaving "home" in what Walter Brueggemann describes as "a dangerous departure from the presumed world of norms and security." He even daringly suggests that the whole of the Abrahamic narrative is premised on a seeming contradiction: to stay in safety is to remain barren; to leave in risk is to have hope.[4]

Although Abraham was obedient to the call he received, it's somehow comforting to remember that he was not without hesitation. He asks the question many of us have asked: "How am I to know?" (Gen. 15:6–8). We want to know whether we are doing the right thing. We want to know if what we hear is truly God's call and not just our own ego whispering lies.

Unfortunately, God's answer to Abraham did not help much. It was terrifyingly ambiguous, all about three-year-old goats and turtledoves and split carcasses and birds of prey. It's not surprising that "a deep and terrifying darkness" fell on Abraham. Could that darkness be a metaphor for the kind of anxiety we sometimes experience when we are called to journey down strange roads? The good news is that, in the midst of this darkness, Abraham received God's assurance of emancipation and prosperity for his offspring and "peace" and "a good old age" for him. The darkness was defeated by the presence of God in the symbol of fire. The covenant was renewed and Abraham's call verified. Our moments of hesitation and dark doubt may not be resolved by flaming torches passing between chunks of goat and pigeon, but this story reminds us that if we possess patience, humility, and openness, resolution will come.

There are many other stories of hesitant responses to God's call. Moses claimed he was no good at public speaking; Jeremiah said he was "only a boy." Jonah ran away to Tarshish. But then there was Isaiah, who said, "Here am I; send me!" and Paul, whose life was immediately and dramatically changed when he heard God's call. Paul wrote about that experience using unforgettable road language: "This one thing I do: forgetting what lies behind and straining forward to what lies ahead, I press on toward the goal for the prize of the heavenly call of God in Christ Jesus" (Phil. 3:13–14).

We find ourselves reflected in these varied responses. When God's call comes to us, we are not always ready to step out on that unknown road. Perhaps a part of our reluctance stems from the realization that God's call to us is always a call to service. Paul's own account of his conversion (Gal. 1:13–17) combines both the call "through . . . grace" and the call to proclaim that grace. When God's call comes to us, creating "holy discomfort" within us, we respond by setting out on new roads, new opportunities for service. It means remembering that "to stay in safety is to remain barren, to leave in risk is to have hope." It summons us to leave home with the same joyous spirit of anticipation expressed in this ancient Celtic prayer:

> Let us go forth,
> In the wisdom of our all-seeing Father,
> In the patience of our all-loving brother,
> In the truth of the all knowing Spirit,
> In the learning of the apostles,
> In the gracious guidance of the angels,
> In the patience of the saints,
> In the self-control of the martyrs.
> Such is the path for all servants of Christ,
> The path from death to eternal life.[5]

LEAVING HOME AS SELF-DISCOVERY

A part of the thrill of the open road comes from the knowledge that leaving home can be a time of self-discovery. We have a chance to find out who we really are when we step away from previous roles. Almost all studies that have been done about how mature faith develops, for example, point to the need for a time of separation from inherited faith in order to truly "own" faith. (See James Fowler's *Stages of Faith* and John Westerhoff's *Will Our Children Have Faith?* for a more detailed description of the various stages of faith development.) Although Fowler describes that time of separation as "a frightening and somewhat disorienting time of being apart from one's conventional moorings,"[6] it can also be a time for the discovery of a new identity. In her luminous book on the spiritual life, *Soul Feast*, Marjorie Thompson echoes that thought: "Each of us needs to grow out of second-hand faith to a knowledge of the way the Spirit works in our own lives."[7]

For many, that distancing occurs with the physical act of leaving home. That may mean leaving the parental home to go away to college or move into an apartment, or it may be leaving familiar surroundings because of a death, a divorce, financial setbacks, or natural disasters. Physical dislocations can be devastating, or they can provide a sense of freedom, independence, and self-control. They may be instruments of genuine psychological or spiritual self-discovery.

Many well-loved works of fiction incorporate this theme of self-discovery, unrelated to age. Suzanne Rahn, in her fascinating study of L. Frank Baum's books, *The Wizard of Oz: Shaping an Imaginary World,* suggests that Dorothy's story is one of self-discovery, "in which Dorothy comes to realize her own potential by journey's end. In this interpretation, the Scarecrow, the Tin Woodsman, and the Cowardly Lion represent not only the friends we all need to help us on our way but also the qualities Baum felt were most essential for the traveler—qualities that Dorothy is to find within herself."[8] Rahn feels that Baum was intentionally trying to encourage children, who were just beginning their life journeys, to discover their own strengths.

The Bible has a distinctive perspective on self-discovery. It is not so much about our discovering ourselves as an act of will as it is about being led to discovery of ourselves by God. That self-discovery is guided by the Torah, by the words of the prophets, by the teachings of Jesus, and by the guidance of the Holy Spirit. The self is never left to its own vague, amorphous conclusions about what it should be. An instruction manual is provided, and true self-discovery occurs when we follow its directions.

Jacob's Transformation

A central image in Scripture is that of a wandering, pilgrim people guided by their God toward a new understanding of themselves. Nowhere is this image more vividly presented than in the story of Jacob at the ford of the Jabbok River in Genesis 32. This encounter provides a fascinating portrayal of the role God plays in self-discovery. Jacob's metamorphosis begins with an intimidating experience of threat and injury, but the threat is transformed mysteriously into an experience of growth. The metamorphosis is revealed in the change in Jacob's name. In ancient times, it was believed that selfhood was expressed in the name given a person. Jacob's new name signified his new self. No longer was he the "Supplanter," or "trickster." He became "Israel," a name that bears one of the names of God, "El," and probably means "God rules."

What happened to Jacob at Jabbok? First, let's recall Jacob's story. He had left his adopted home in Haran, where he had married Leah and Rachel and had tricked his Uncle Laban out of a goodly portion of his wealth, so that he could return home to Canaan with his family. Laban pursued him hotly, and he and Jacob declared an uneasy truce on the heights of Gilead in the Transjordan. Jacob then followed the King's Highway to the Jabbok River cleft. He and his entourage made the almost five-thousand-foot descent to the ford, where Jacob paused to divide his flock into two companies. He did this because he was on his way to meet his estranged brother Esau after twenty years, and was fearful that Esau might try to destroy his flocks, stripping him of his wealth. By dividing the companies, one might survive an attack. He also sent gifts to Esau to gain his favor. Then, after seeing his family safely across the Jabbok ford, Jacob stayed behind and had the strange encounter that changed his life.

Jacob's transformation was not a peaceful one. He was assaulted and attacked, not by evil forces, but by God. "A man," who later identifies himself as God (Gen. 32:28) wrestles with Jacob all night, finally putting his hip out of joint. Sometimes God's grace can feel like an assault. Its very nature challenges our ideas about who we are and what is important, and it is never comfortable to be challenged. The Jacob who had embarked on this journey was filled with anger and mistrust toward his father-in-law and fear of his brother Esau. He had already encountered angels on the road, a reminder that the power of God was working in his life. As the psalm says, "The angel of the Lord encamps / around those who fear him, and delivers them" (Ps. 34:7). Jacob doesn't know it, but he is about to be delivered.

In that wrestling match with God, Jacob shows his tenacity and his strength. He faced God, he was touched by God, he gained a blessing from God, and he was changed by God. In that sense, Jacob's story is one of self-discovery through the grace of God. He became a new person, not because he deserved God's mercy, but because of unmerited grace.

And the result? After meeting God "face to face" (v. 30) Jacob is able, amazingly, to see "the face of God" in the face of his brother, whom he had feared and hated (Gen. 33:10). Jacob's transformation by the power of God made reconciliation with his brother possible.

Saul's Transformation

In the New Testament, Acts 9 has a similar road story of an individual's discovery of true self through God's grace. The zealous Pharisee Saul was traveling the Damascus Road "breathing threats and murder" against the radical sect known as followers of the Way. Saul was carrying with him letters of extradition, so that he might forcibly retrieve followers of the Way who had left their homes in Jerusalem to seek refuge in Damascus. He wanted to "bring them bound" to stand trial in Jerusalem for heresy. It was a long trip: seventy-five miles on the Hill Road to Galilee, where the road intersected with the Via Maris and continued for another forty-five miles to Damascus. Somewhere on that road, Saul's journey was abruptly interrupted. A light from heaven flashed around him and he heard the voice of the One whose followers he was persecuting (Acts 9:1–5).

As a result of this encounter, Saul became God's "chosen instrument." The process of transformation from persecutor to believer must, like Jacob's, have felt like an assault from God, even though there was no wrestling. Both Saul and Jacob were disabled. Jacob's hip was put out of joint; Saul was blinded. Jacob received a new name and a new identity after his ordeal, and, in a sense, Saul did too. He was no longer a "Pharisee of the Pharisees," but a follower of the Way. Both Jacob and Saul were given new vocations. Jacob became a revered and respected leader of his people. Saul was commissioned "to be a minister of Christ Jesus to the Gentiles" (Rom. 15:16).

Leaving home to discover one's true self by the gift of God's grace can lead us down new roads into new adventures.

LEAVING HOME: A PAINFUL BREAK AND A SCARY RISK

When John Donne wrote, in "The Legacy," "When I died last, and dear, I die, / as often as from thee I go," he was acknowledging that leaving involves grieving, a sense of loss, and, in many ways, a kind of death. The fear of loss can be so overwhelming that it can even make us want to stay home, to ignore the lure of the road, to hide in the womb of the familiar. We are like two-year-olds, balanced precariously between crying out, "I want to do it myself" and, "Take care of me."

The pain of leaving home is assuaged by trust, by being willing, as Abraham and Sarah were, to leave the past behind and go out on the road in spite of the pain and grief. We may leave home with tears in our eyes, but the grief can turn to joy when we trust the One who is our guide.

> The LORD will keep
> your going out and your coming in
> from this time on and forevermore.
> (Ps. 121:8)

The Exiles in Babylon

Old Testament scholar Walter Brueggemann describes in *Cadences of Home* how the exiles on the road to Babylon experienced "a loss of the structured, reliable world which gave them meaning and coherence."[9] Their pain at this loss is expressed memorably in Psalm 137:

> By the rivers of Babylon—
>> there we sat down and there we wept
>> when we remembered Zion.
>>> (Ps. 137:1)

The Babylonian exile actually consisted of three deportations of Jews to Babylon. An account of the first deportation, in 597 B.C., is given in 2 Kings 24:12–16, which describes the captivity of King Jehoiachin and his retinue and thousands of others, so that "no one remained, except the poorest people of the land" (v. 14). The second deportation was in 587, after the destruction of the Temple and the walls of the city. The third was in 582 as a Babylonian reprisal for the assassination of Governor Gedaliah by a Jewish nationalist faction. The exile lasted until the edict of Cyrus in 538 permitted the return of the exiles. There is no way to know exactly how many were taken to Babylonia, but the assessment of all "except the poorest" is probably accurate, for dislocation was a favorite strategy for curbing the possibility of revolt.

The poignancy of Psalm 137, as well as the wrenching poetry of Lamentations, describes the pain of a people whose sense of meaning and coherence had been linked to the Temple, the powerful symbol of God's presence among them. The loss of that special place was even more painful than the loss of their homes and the routines of a stable life.

In contemporary church life, the loss of meaning and coherence is a very real issue. Liturgies change, new hymnals are purchased, familiar prayers and music are replaced by the unfamiliar, new justice issues are constantly surfacing. All of these constitute painful breaks with the "way things have always been done" and are often the occasion of resentment, frustration, and even anger. I remember a retired missionary's words at a missions conference in the '80s: "What's all this talk about peace and justice? Whatever happened to the good old days when we went out into the world to preach the gospel?" She was at home with a certain language about missions, and traveling down new roads of terminology was unsettling and even frightening. She felt that the old, secure basis for evangelism was slipping away, despite the fact that this language came directly from the prophets and from Jesus himself.

The irony is that the kingdom of heaven is sometimes sabotaged by Christian service. We build structures in order to serve God. The problem comes when those structures become rigid, calcified, sacred. There's truth in the saying that the seven last words of the church will be "But we have never done that before."

Jesus' Homelessness

One of Jesus' most poignant utterances is found only in Matthew and Luke:

> "Foxes have holes, and birds of the air have nests; but the Son of Man has nowhere to lay his head."
>
> (Luke 9:58; Matt. 8:20)

In Matthew, he says this after the Sermon on the Mount during his visit to Capernaum (Matt. 8:20). In Luke, its timing is even more dramatic. It occurs during what is generally called the Perean ministry of Jesus, on his way to Jerusalem. It follows the transfiguration, the second mention of the passion and the disciples' lack of understanding, the rejection of Jesus by the Samaritans, and a statement indicating what one commentator has aptly described as "the unswerving intensity, the destiny-oriented sense of Jesus' move toward Jerusalem":[10] "When the days drew near for him to be taken up, he set his face to go to Jerusalem" (Luke 9:51). It is after the enthusiastic offer from one of Jesus' followers (Matthew calls him "a scribe") to follow him "wherever he goes," that Jesus speaks those pain-filled words of homelessness.

With this vivid expression, Jesus implies that those who follow him must be prepared for rejection, for a painful break with family and friends, with the religious establishment, and with their communities. Even "the Son of Man" had nowhere to lay his head. This is certainly not what his followers wanted to hear. Then, to make matters worse, Jesus seems to read their minds about the excuses they were conjuring up. I once read a tongue-in-cheek article in a church publication called "Why I Can't Possibly Help You Out Just Now," which offered "all-purpose reasons you can use for why you can't do it, whatever it is." This is not a new idea. Jesus' followers found similar excuses to avoid making what seemed to them to be a painful break with safety and security.

Jesus wanted his followers to understand that following him means change. Sometimes this does mean a painful break with the way things have always been done. That painful break, however, can lead to a renewal of the ability to sense the wind of the Spirit, and a renewal of a living and dynamic relationship with our God. We use the word "dynamic" casually, but it has its origin in the Greek word *dynamis*, meaning "power." In the Christian community, the power to change, to make a break with the past, comes from the Holy Spirit. The activity of the Spirit is not the preservation of the status quo, but newness, change, vitality, and transformation. This power enables us to be what God wants us to be. Through the Spirit, we see where changes need to be made; through the Spirit we receive the power to make those changes. The call of the gospel is to "live the future," as painful as it is to let the past go.

Taking the Risk

At a time in my life when I was reluctant to make a break with the familiar to start down a new road, I wrote a poem to express my anxiety. It began this way:

I am bird frail
    fluttering on the rim of straw
    knowing that a fall
    may be instantly fatal.
My untried wings
    test airs with fear
    slicing the clouds
    to find security.

> I am hovering here
>   cautiously
>   above daisies and stones
>   looking at downs and sinking.[11]

Walter Brueggemann's statement, which I noted earlier, that to leave in risk is to have hope, is not an easy one to accept. We hover on our "rims of straw," or peek anxiously out of our doors, preferring safety to risk. I wish I could say I have completely overcome the fear of risk and now always look forward eagerly to new challenges. But the truth is that "leaving home," whether that means a new venture, a new vocation, or a new domicile, still fills me with panic. At one point, when I began a new job, I moaned, "Why did I ever think I could do this? I'm scared to death." My daughter responded with a sigh: "Oh, Mom, you always say that!"

She's right. I always do. The thought of stepping out into the unknown makes me "test airs with fear." And yet, when I finally leave the nest, or set foot on the yellow brick road that stretches out before me, I sense again the lure of the road and the thrill of discovery. When the fear of leaving home for new roads overtakes me, I post this beautiful reminder of the help I have had in past journeys: "God carried you, just as one carries a child, all the way that you traveled until you reached this place" (Deut. 1:31).

LEAVING HOME AS AN ACT OF REBELLION

There is another kind of leaving home testified to in Scripture: an act of defiance and rebellion. This leaving may begin in eagerness, but it ends in despair and desperation. When my sister, Jeanie, was about six or seven, she was punished by Mother for some minor misdemeanor. In a spirit of rebellion, Jeanie pulled from her closet four or five of her little dresses, still on their hangers, and struck out. She got as far as the corner of our front yard, when her eagerness evaporated and despair took over. She sank down sobbing on her heap of dresses, until Mother came to her rescue and led her gently back into the house.

The Lost Boy

A similar but more tragic illustration of leaving home in rebellion is found in Jesus' parable of the lost boy. Henri Nouwen has written a wonderful book of reflections on Rembrandt's painting *The Return of the Prodigal Son.* In commenting on the story, Nouwen says that the son's leaving is actually a heartless rejection of the home in which he was nurtured and a break with the tradition of his community. His asking for his inheritance while his father was still living was the same as wishing his father dead.[12]

It's easy for us to associate the son's action with the way young people leave behind, temporarily or permanently, the traditions and values of their parents. It's not so easy, however, to recognize our own rebelliousness. We take all kinds of strange roads because we have left the arms that shelter and embrace us. We turn our backs on friends, family, tradition, and inherited values. Sometimes, the result may be true self-discovery, as we have already seen. Healthy questioning can lead to a real appreciation of inherited traditions and values. But it can also lead to living in pigsties in far countries.

Rebellion and Loss of Meaning

One of the prevalent sicknesses of our day is the loss of meaning. Theologian Douglas John Hall suggests that the primal anxiety of contemporary North Americans is not guilt before God and fear of eternal damnation but, in Paul Tillich's terms, "the anxiety of meaninglessness and despair."[13] In biblical understanding, meaninglessness and despair are the result of abandoning the law of God, a particular kind of rebellious "leaving home." Righteousness and lawlessness are mutually exclusive. The First Letter of John is emphatic: "To commit sin is to break God's law: sin, in fact, is lawlessness" (1 John 3:4 TEV). Lawlessness or sin is nothing other than rebellion or revolt against God.

Like the prodigal son, we leave home, mad at rules, mad at tradition, mad at God. We think we can do better on our own. We leave home and get as far as the corner of the yard, or maybe even as far as a distant country, and suddenly there is nothing left but meaninglessness and emptiness.

The point of the parable, however, is that even rebellion may be an instrument of grace. The son's rebellion led him to discover what was real and what was illusion. The road away from home can always be the road back, and the parable reminds us vividly that no matter how rebellious we've been, we have a Father who waits for us with outstretched arms.

CONCLUSION

Over and over again in this life, we leave home. We leave it with a sense of adventure, responding to the lure of the road. We leave it to discover ourselves. We leave it grieving for the loss of the familiar, the comfortable, the known, for dear places and faces we must leave behind. We leave it, full of fear of what lies ahead, not really wanting to face it. We leave the home where we truly belong in a spirit of rebellion, wanting to have it all, wanting no handed-down laws, no stale rules, no stuffy traditions. We reject the One who loves us best but the good news is, home is still there, waiting for us. God's love is steadfast, protecting us in our going out . . . and in our coming in.

I concluded my poem about leaving the nest in this way:

> If I dared trust
>   the tiny infinite hollows of feathers
>   to brace me up
>   I'd soar into the sun.
> Is there strength enough
>   in grace?
> Is the secure swoop possible
>   even for me?
> I will give my life to it!
> AWAY
> UPWARD
> GLIDE THE WIND![14]

The Bible is about journeys and pilgrims who embark on those journeys, people who were willing to leave home, who took a chance that there is strength in grace and gave their lives to it. Their stories give us courage to set bravely out from home and face the road ahead with eager feet.

GUIDEPOSTS FOR YOUR JOURNEY

1. What is your earliest recollection of leaving home? How did it feel? Was it a joyful adventure or a painful break? Was it a time of self-discovery? What did you learn about yourself?
2. Write a cinquain about feelings you have when you set out on a journey. In a cinquain, the first line contains the title (one word); the second describes the title (two words); the third line contains action words or a phrase (three words); the fourth contains feeling words related to the title (four words); the fifth line is the conclusion (one word).
3. Does one of the biblical stories about leaving home discussed in this chapter connect with your own life experience? In what way?
4. When have you felt God calling you down a new road? What was your response? List the resources that helped you make that response (Scripture, prayer, conversations with others, community worship, and so on).

3   ON THE ROAD AGAIN

Coping with Change

By faith he stayed for a time in the land he had been promised,
as in a foreign land, living in tents."

—Hebrews 11:9

Life is its own journey, presupposes its own change and movement, and one tries
to arrest them at one's eternal peril.

—Laurens Van der Post, 1951

Future shock . . . the shattering stress and disorientation that we induce in individuals by subjecting them to too much change in too short a time.

—Alvin Toffler, 1970

Roads imply change. They take us from deserts to mountains, from towns to
cities, from farmlands to wildernesses, from the known to the unknown. Who
knows what terror hides around the next bend in the road? Who knows what mag-
nificent vistas will thrill us from the crest of the next hill? That terror and that thrill
are a part of the lure of the road.

Change can be wonderful and refreshing, providing a burst of renewed energy.
Tourist agencies use this rationale to sell vacations in Tuscany or the Bahamas.
Change can also be wrenching and devastating, leaving us feeling helpless in the
face of the strenuous adjustments demanded of us. For this reason, change is not

always welcomed. There is a comfort in the sameness and predictability of not having to face either terror or thrill.

The reality is, however, that as much as people might wish that things would stay the same, they never do. A few years ago, I visited the small South Carolina town of Belton, in which I spent my growing-up years. It was going home to a "quasi familiarity." Many of my childhood landmarks had disappeared: the high school from which I graduated, the old hotel, the stately mansion of "Miss Elinor" on our street, the woods behind our house where bluets grew, the building where my father worked. There were unsettling changes in other places that had framed my life: our two-story family home had been "upgraded" with a brick facade and columns, losing its cool front porch in the process. A "For Sale" sign stood in front of the church in which I was married. Homes of my friends had worn frail after years of sheltering their families. I found that I resented all these changes and wanted to put everything back into the shape of the Belton I remembered. Change happens whether we like it or not.

The times we live in have brought dramatic changes that have left many of us feeling as uprooted as the exiles in Babylon, separated from all that feels safe and familiar. Like Alice in Wonderland, we feel that we have to run as fast as we can just to stay in the same place. My Aunt Robbie died in January 2001, at age one hundred and three. At her funeral her grandson, Don, spoke these words: "She lived in three centuries, seeing everything from the first telephone, gas cars, commercial airlines, world wars, space exploration, antibiotics, gas heating, air conditioning, and the first presidential recount."

Amazingly, Don failed to mention computers, which have probably accelerated change in the way we transact everyday affairs more rapidly than any other single invention. In fact, the world of the computer changes so fast that the host of a computer information show on National Public Radio signs off each week with these words: "Just remember, everything you heard on this show today will be obsolete by next week." Trying to keep up with the mind-boggling technology of our day gives us the uneasy feeling that we are living in tents, as Abraham did, on the shifting sands of a constantly changing desert. Religious groups are rushing online, setting up church home pages, broadcasting dogma and establishing theological newsgroups, bulletin boards, and chat rooms. Thousands discuss over the Internet religious topics about which they are tongue-tied in public. Churches that don't establish a presence in cyberspace fear that they may soon be out of touch with their congregations. A new form of scholarship called "hypertheology" uses the Internet to connect religious documents of different faiths, and *Time* magazine reports, "We stand at the start of a new movement in this delicate dance of technology and faith: the marriage of God and the global computer networks. There's no sure way to measure how much the Internet will change our lives, but the most basic truth about technological revolutions is that they change everything they touch."[1]

Change affects our most cherished cultural institutions. The image of what constitutes the typical American family has been shattered. Rapid changes have left us stunned and bewildered: half of all marriages ending in divorce; the increasing number of children in single-parent families; latchkey kids, youth caught up in a vortex of changing mores and values. The news stories that bombard us about our children are tragic: fourth-graders addicted to drugs, preteens killing their classmates in planned attacks, a rising tide of unwed mothers. These problems are not limited to any social or economic group, and the church is not exempt. A 1990 survey of mainstream churches revealed some frightening statistics about youth who are active in church: 80 percent of eleventh- and twelfth-graders and 66 percent of seventh- and eighth-graders confessed to having at least one "at risk" factor in their lives, including depression, suicide, alcohol use, binge drinking, drugs, unprotected sex, or theft.[2]

The spiritual climate of our nation has undergone seismic changes in the last decade. The disintegration of biblical literacy has led us onto some strange roads: New Age spirituality, a passion for angels, quasi-inspirational *Chicken Soup* stories substituting for biblical curriculum in churches, and apocalyptic novels heading the best-seller lists. We opt for an individualistic, self-centered approach to spirituality that ignores the community-centered nature of the gospel and treats faith as if it were a self-help manual to prosperity and success. One researcher has found that at least 20 percent of the public ardently believe in astrology and 40 percent admit they talk to the dead. According to Gerald Celente, who runs the Trends Research Institute in Rhinebeck, New York, "What's happening now is unprecedented in modern times. Because people lack optimism, we see astrology believers increasing, more religious converts, more cults, more sightings of ghosts."[3] He finds increasing angst, especially among baby boomers, many of whom are desperate for "meaning in life." He also maintains that interest in meditation, voodoo, New Age beliefs, even UFOs, is also rising. It is interesting that he lists religious conversion as just another evidence of "lack [of] optimism"!

The church in the twenty-first century finds itself in the midst of rapid changes that call into question its very nature and meaning. Only 43 percent of the American public remain in the religious body into which they were born.[4] The result is a lack of a cohesive denominational theology and identity. This doctrinal confusion, combined with the rising tide of biblical illiteracy, makes it extremely difficult for churches to deal with today's enormous issues: abortion, homosexuality, the separation of church and state, genetic research, ecological exploitation, school massacres, and the disintegrating structures of family and society. Committed Christians face each other—sometimes with hostility—from opposite sides of divisive issues, trying to discern which changes are in line with God's will and purpose.

We are learning the hard truth of the statement made by South African writer Laurens Van der Post, that life presupposes change and movement and we try to stop them at our peril. For the church, the questions raised by movement and change are important ones. How does the church survive in times of rapid change? How can it hear the voice of God in the midst of the rapid-fire changes that are thrust upon it? How can it witness to the unchanging gospel message with clarity and compassion? What help can we gain from biblical stories of change?

THE CHANGING WORLD OF THE BIBLE

Change is not new. Indeed, it is one of the most powerful and pervasive themes in Scripture. The "one story" of the Bible is a story of what it means to move from being "no people" to being "God's people." That story of movement and change begins "in the beginning," with the account of Adam and Eve's move from paradise into a radically changed existence of toil and thorns and thistles and sweat. It continues with the movements of the patriarchs, to whom change was an everyday reality. Their descendants moved from Egypt to the wilderness to long-awaited "good land." The period of Israel's settling into that land was a time of violent change. The establishment of the monarchy represented a dramatic change of structure, designed to bring order out of reigning chaos. The map of the world of the Hebrew Bible was drawn over and over again as nations toppled nations. Famine and flood changed people's destinies. The movement into exile was a change so disruptive that it could have destroyed the Israelites' sense of who they were. Instead, it shaped and defined it. Over and over again, the prophets sounded the call to change: "Change your ways! Return to your God! Repent!"

The message of Jesus was, like that of the prophets, a call to radical change. He opened people's eyes to a new understanding of God and God's laws. He challenged them to begin the movement toward a new life of faith, appropriately called "the Way." The lives of Jesus' disciples were changed as they began to understand what that meant. The writings of Paul are filled with the motifs of change and newness. The book of Revelation provides hope for the final glorious day of change, which will create "a new heaven and a new earth," where there will be no death or tears or mourning.

When we read these old, old stories, we realize that God does not endorse the status quo. Our God is a moving God, a whirlwind, who stirs us into motion, keeps us restless, implants in us that holy discomfort that keeps us "on the road again."

LIVING IN TENTS

The Patriarchs

The long journey of Abraham and Sarah began when they left the ancient city of Ur in lower Mesopotamia with Abraham's father, Terah. They traveled to Haran, in the northern part of the Mesopotamian valley. Research in biblical geography suggests that they were probably a part of a large migration movement that took place as a general urban collapse occurred in the Fertile Crescent.[5] As early as two centuries before Abraham, the great city of Ur had lost much of its political and economic power. As a result, times became hard for merchants and traders, who began to leave home for greener economic fields.

After Terah's death in Haran, Abraham received a call to leave home, and thereby to break the ties of land and kindred to play a decisive role in God's plans. Passages such as Isaiah 51:2 acknowledge that role:

> Look to Abraham your father,
>   and to Sarah who bore you;
> for he was but one when I called him,
>   but I blessed him and made him many.

With Abraham's call, he and Sarah entered into lives of constant change. The three words in Hebrews 11:9, "living in tents," describe their lifestyle as one of change, movement, and no permanence. For years, biblical scholars assumed that the patriarchs were pastoral nomads, like the bedouins of today, but recent studies maintain that the wanderings of the patriarchs were done for other reasons. One Old Testament scholar, Norman K. Gottwald, suggests that "the movements of the ancestors are largely explained as historically caused migrations for purposes of change of residence, religious pilgrimage, strife with outsiders, securing wives, escaping famine, and the like, rather than due to the regular seasonal movements of pastoral nomads."[6] There are references in Scripture, however, that indicate that some members of the patriarchs' families did take flocks into favorable seasonal pasturage while the rest of the family stayed in more permanent settlements. Joseph's brothers went seventy-five miles north of the family home at Hebron to Dothan "to pasture their father's flock" (Gen. 37:12). It was there that his brothers conspired to kill him, then instead to sell him to the Ishmaelite traders on their way to Egypt.

Israel never forgot its tent-life origins. The word "Hebrew" itself (as it is used in Genesis 14:13 to describe Abraham) may actually mean "wanderer." The Psalms, the Song of Solomon, Isaiah, and Jeremiah are filled with nostalgic allusions to wandering and living in tents, such as this one from Isaiah:

> Look on Zion, the city of our appointed festivals!
>   Your eyes will see Jerusalem,
>   a quiet habitation, an immovable tent,
> whose stakes will never be pulled up,
>   and none of whose ropes will be broken.
>
> Isa. 33:20

The prophets frequently contrasted the virtue of a simple tent lifestyle to the sinfulness of city mores. Jeremiah, for instance, praised the Rechabites, a group dedicated to rootless, mobile lives, and told the inhabitants of Jerusalem they could learn a lesson from their lives of simplicity and obedience (Jer. 35:5–19).

Tenting Today

One poignant expression of the strangeness of our contemporary world is the increased mobility of its populations. Several years ago I read that the average American moves seven times in adulthood. It is no longer unusual to relocate because of job opportunities, family needs, or retirement. Serial homes, serial friends, and rootlessness have become "the American way of life." In our cities, rapidly burgeoning subdivisions, moving vans, and "For Sale" signs are a common sight.

My husband and I passed the number seven long ago. We knew that the life to which we had been called as missionaries in the Congo would necessitate change. In fact, we looked forward to the excitement of a mobile lifestyle with eagerness and enthusiasm. We never realized, however, just how mobile it would be. Living between two continents has meant that since we were married we have moved thirty-one times. Thirty-one instances of radical change: leaving home, starting over in a new place, making adjustments to a new life. Our oldest son, Eric, was a junior in college when he wrote home: "I've just realized that this is the first time in my life that I've been in the same school more than two consecutive years." When retirement came close, Dan and I faced the stern reality of these questions: Where do we put down roots? Where is home? We had lived in tents for so long that we had no permanent place of belonging.

We all know similar stories of people who say, "I never thought in my wildest dreams I'd be moving around the way I have." If it has not happened to us, it has happened to our children, or to our friends. We have become a nation of wanderers. While we don't literally live in tents, we have adopted the same sort of mobile existence as Abraham and his heirs.

Living in tents can be hazardous to your health. In 1971, Dr. Thomas Holmes, professor of psychiatry at the University of Washington in Seattle, developed a "life events scale" to measure the psychological stress that can be caused by various changes in life's circumstances. He gave the death of a spouse a rating of 100 points; divorce, 73; marriage, 50; retirement, 45; change to a different line of work, 36; change in residence, 20; and even Christmas, 12. He found that too many changes, coming too close together, often produce grave illness or abysmal depression.[7]

So the question is, how do we cope with change? What clues can we gain from the patriarchs' stories that can help us hold down our tents in the face of the winds of change? Two passages in the Letter to the Hebrews about the story of Abraham speak to this in a powerful way:

> By faith [Abraham] stayed for a time in the land he had been promised, as in a foreign land, living in tents, as did Isaac and Jacob, who were heirs with him of the same promise. For he looked forward to the city that has foundations, whose architect and builder is God.
>
> (Heb. 11:9–10)

> If they had been thinking of the land that they had left behind, they would have had opportunity to return.
>
> (Heb. 11:15)

Abraham survived amid a lifestyle of mobility and change because he did not look back with longing to "the way things used to be," but kept focused on the possibilities of the future and the sure promises of the God who was leading him by the hand. Abraham's story reminds us that we can not only remain alive in the midst of change; we can be fulfilled by it. The effect of change on us depends on where our focus is, on what we love most. If we love ourselves selfishly, change is hateful and has to be avoided at all costs. We like the way we are, and we want to stay that way. If we love God and love others in God, we will be glad to let change destroy anything in us that keeps us from expressing that love.

When we left our lives as missionaries in the Congo, the transition to life in the States was a very difficult one for me. I had not wanted to leave my work and my African friends. Arriving in a university town in the late '60s was a genuine culture shock. The dress, music, and mores of the countercultural movement with which we were surrounded were a far cry from the lifestyle we had known as missionaries. We had little money and few possessions. My husband's salary as a teaching assistant did not quite cover our basic living expenses. We had to acclimate our four children, who had been home-schooled in Africa, to the American public school system. We were starting life all over again, but under these circumstances it was not easy.

Then someone shared with me a quotation that helped me put the changes in my life in perspective: "Change is only a moment's pain between familiarity and familiarity." I realized that although the changes God brings into our lives may be painful at the time, that pain does not have to last. It simply marks the moment of transition between the old securities to which we want to cling and the new freedoms that will become familiar through the gift of grace. The gift of grace enables us to see change as a positive happening, to accept and even cherish it. If we keep thinking of the land we left behind, change will be nothing but misery. If we look forward "to the city that has foundations," we will recognize that change does not have to be catastrophic, but can be an occasion for great joy.

Many of the changes the church has faced through the years have been occasions of pain: the acceptance of Gentiles, the acceptance of people of all races, the acceptance of women. In each transition, there were those who kept looking back with longing to "the land left behind," who felt that these changes in church traditions and polity were, indeed, catastrophic. But there were others who, like the patriarchs, looked forward to a city "whose architect and builder is God," where there is no discrimination, prejudice, and hatred. These decisions were moments of pain for the church, but now we can see them as the gift of grace. John Calvin taught that order was a good gift of God that comes to us in different ways. But he also believed in change: that we are free to adapt and transform tradition as necessary to carry out God's purposes in a changing world. This view of order is rooted in the slogan of the Reformed Church: "Reformed and always reforming."

Like the patriarchs, the church must keep focused on its true goal as it lives in the tents of change. That goal is the kingdom of God. Like the patriarchs, the church can move through difficult changes "by faith," under the guidance of the One who brings it safely through all kinds of trouble.

FROM NO PEOPLE TO GOD'S PEOPLE

The Covenant

Moses' life is a study in change. He left the luxurious palaces of Egypt for a wandering life in a rocky wilderness. He led his people across the Red Sea, guided them along unknown roads, and took them to the very threshold of the land they had been promised, the goal of all their road wanderings. The exodus from Egypt, the wilderness wanderings, and the settlement into Canaan contributed to an astonishing change in the people Moses had shepherded out of Egypt.

But it was the covenant given to Moses, spelled out in the Torah or Law, that gave form, shape, and definition to their new identity as "God's people." It showed them, as Walter Brueggemann explains, "how to order life in new modes."[8]

When the Israelites came out of Egypt, they had an identity problem. Who were they indeed? Slaves and descendants of slaves. Nobodies. Did they all worship the one true God? Hardly. Did they know exactly where they were going and why? Hardly. Did they all believe and trust in Moses as their fearless leader? Hardly. They grumbled and complained and wanted to go back to leeks and onions and depose Moses and put up a calf to worship, something they could see and believe in. The promise to Abraham had been made two thousand years earlier, and although it had been retold many times, it was pretty remote. The Israelites needed to know who they were, and what the God of cloud and fire who had led them out of Egypt expected of them.

The covenant gave them identity by defining the responsibilities of being God's people, by providing a set of rules that showed them how God wanted them to live. Georgia Harkness once commented, "A good God demands goodness." The law defined that "goodness." It provided a "people of God handbook."

The covenant was also a centripetal force uniting a group of assorted tribes that were quite likely to spin off in their own directions. If there was ever a nation founded on the phrase "This nation, under God," it was Israel. God was their leader, their ruler, their commander in chief, their king, through all the changes facing them. It was God who molded them from "no people" into "God's people."

Becoming the People of God

God's law continues to provide structure for our lives in the midst of traumatic changes. It continues to be a searching spotlight, a pitiless mirror that shows us where we fall short. When we don't like what we see, we have to admit we are not living as God's people. It calls us to change, to be what we are supposed to be. However, being the people of God means we live in the light of grace. The God who tells us how to change forgives us when we fail to do so and lets us begin again. Julian of Norwich said it well: "If there be anywhere on earth a lover of God who is always kept safe from falling, I know nothing of it . . . for it was not shown me. But this was shown: that in falling and rising again we are always held close in one love."[9]

When we see the law in this perspective, we can understand how the psalmist could say, "Oh, how I love your law!" (Ps. 119: 97).

Throughout the Bible, the spiritually alive person is pictured as a person who is willing to change. This is clearly expressed in Hebrews 6:1 (TEV): "Let us go forward, then, to mature teaching and leave behind the first lessons of the Christian message." Without change we will become stagnant pools instead of springs of water "whose waters never fail" (Isa. 58:11).

Real change demands humility and trust. We cannot go on assuming that the old ways are always the best. Neither can we assume that we know everything, that we have all the answers. We have to be willing to face the uncomfortable risks of change in order to grow, to unfold, to be like trees that grow beside a stream, that bear fruit at the right time and prosper (Ps. 1:3). The evening before our grand-daughter, Laura, turned six, her mother found her crying in her room. When she asked Laura why she was crying, Laura said tearfully, "Oh, Mom, I'm not ready to be six. You know how I don't like doing new things!"

I've often felt that way myself. "I'm not ready for this new thing, God!" Change may not be easy, but if we are to find our identity as the children of God, we have to remember that our God is the same God who proclaimed joyously to Isaiah, "I am about to do a new thing" (Isa. 43:19), and "From this time forward I make you hear new things" (48:6). We may not like "doing new things," but our God knows that in that experience we discover new truths about ourselves, and find new joys, new opportunities, and new faith.

REPENTANCE: A CALL TO CHANGE

Repentance in the Old Testament

God calls us to change, to slough off our foolish ways, to become new creatures, to relish challenges. Paradoxically, becoming "new "creatures in biblical thought oftentimes means returning to and reclaiming old values. One of the important words in Scripture about change is the one we translate as "repentance." Although there was no special term for repentance in the Hebrew Bible, the prophets expressed the concept with the Hebrew word *shub*, which means "to turn back," or "to turn around." An example is in Jeremiah 8:4:

> When people fall, do they not get up again?
> If they go astray, do they not turn back?

Shub implies a great deal more than just a slight feeling of regret or remorse. It is a word of dramatic change, of turning away from sin and turning back to God. It embraces a person's whole life, claims a person's whole being.

The prophets understood sin not so much as disbelief in God as a willful turning away from God, a turning away expressed in disobedience to God's laws, unfaithfulness, and ingratitude. Repentance was a turning back, a converting, a return to God, resulting in obedience to God's will and a total orientation of the self toward God. No one has written more forcibly about this orientation than Thomas Merton:

> Sin strikes at the very depth of our personality. It destroys the one reality on which our true character, identity, and happiness depend: our fundamental orientation to God. We are created to will what God wills, to know what He knows, to love what He loves. Sin is the will to do what God does not will, to know what He does not know, to love what He does not love.[10]

Such a total orientation may feel strange in the contemporary world of divided loyalties. People find themselves pulled in so many directions, by so many loyalties—family, friends, jobs, volunteer work, community organizations, political parties—that the idea of being totally oriented toward God sounds curiously archaic and impossible. Perhaps this is why, in some mainstream churches, there is not too much preaching or conversation about "repentance" or "conversion." As a result, the impression is given that those two terms apply only to those outside the church: the agnostics, the atheists, the unbelievers, and those of other faith traditions.

The truth is that most of the prophets' admonitions (except for the reluctant Jonah) were to God's chosen people, those inside the fold who had "turned away," faced in the wrong direction, and wandered down the wrong roads. This is why repentance is not so much a "turning toward" God for the first time, as it is a "turning back" to the God whose paths we have abandoned. This is particularly clear in the words of the prophets Amos, Hosea, and Isaiah, in passages such as this: "Come, let us return to the LORD; for it is he who has torn, and he will heal us" (Hos. 6:1). Amos takes a more negative approach. He provides a graphic portrayal of the punishment God meted out to Israel because it "did not return to me" (Amos 4:8). Amos sets forth a clear picture of the urgency of true repentance, of the need to turn back to God with unconditional seriousness.

Repentance in the New Testament

John the Baptist followed in this prophetic tradition of a call to conversion, or turning back to God. The Greek word for repentance is *metanoia,* which literally means changing one's mind or feelings. John's message had a new sense of urgency in the light of the imminent coming of the Messiah. John makes it perfectly clear that the conversion he proclaims is not only for "publicans and sinners," but for everyone, including self-righteous Jews who didn't think they needed it. Like the prophets, John called for a return to life lived according to God's will. John's baptism was a symbol of that "conversion," that turning back, that internal change, that total orientation to God.

Jesus' preaching of conversion goes beyond that of John and the prophets. It is central to his mission. "I have come to call not the righteous but sinners to repentance" (Luke 5:32). In his kingdom, that repentance was not to be accomplished by the ritual acts of penance and self-mortification that had developed in Judaism, but by a total transformation: a radical turning away from evil and a radical turning back to God. The demand for conversion is the one and only imperative in Jesus' preaching of the kingdom of God. It is "addressed to all without distinction and presented with unmitigated severity in order to indicate the only way of salvation there is. It calls for total surrender, total commitment to the will of God."[11]

Paul seldom uses the traditional words for conversion, but the concept is very important to him. He speaks rather of the death of the old person and the rising of the new, of becoming a "new creation," of a new being in Christ: "If anyone is in Christ, there is a new creation: everything old has passed away; see, everything has become new!" (2 Cor. 5:17). He takes the prophetic terminology of turning away from sin and turning back to God and gives it his own special Pauline spin:

> You were taught to put away your former way of life, your old self, corrupt and deluded by its lusts, and to be renewed in the spirit of your minds, and to clothe yourselves with the new self, created according to the likeness of God in true righteousness and holiness.
>
> (Eph. 4:22–24)

His message is not basically different from that of Jesus. It is a call to a transformation made possible by the revelation of God in Christ.

The point of all this is clear. Being made new means reclaiming old values, old allegiances, old obedience. It means change; it means a reorientation to "righteousness and holiness" instead of getting ahead or pleasing others or being rewarded. It means turning back to God, the One from whom we have gone astray down strange roads. It means getting serious about our faith and in the process discovering what it means to be God's people.

The final change anticipated in Scripture is "making all things new" (Rev. 21:5). The apocalyptic vision of John is one of welcome change: there will be "a new heaven and a new earth," creation transformed into what God always intended it should be. There will be a "new Jerusalem," which will offer, in Eugene Boring's phrase, "the fulfillment of all human dreams for the community and security of life in an ideal city."[12] John's wonderful imagery is designed to make us recognize that our God has the power to bring about changes that incorporate our deepest desires: no more tears, death, sorrow, crying, or pain.

CONCLUSION

A friend of mine told me about seeing a bumper sticker that read: "All who wander are not lost." When we find ourselves on the road again, it doesn't mean we are lost. We believe that our wandering is watched over by the One who is its initiator. We believe that God's steadfast love guides us through the changes and "new things" we find on that road. We believe that our journey ends in the embrace of the One who created the path and beckons us to follow it, even if it means living in tents along the way.

Therefore, our response to the movement and changes of life should be gratitude and praise. New roads offer new challenges and new opportunities for growth. They prevent us from being stale and stagnant. The stress of change does not have to be shattering or disorienting. Because we are God's people, we can boldly move on, pitching our tents a day's march nearer home.

GUIDEPOSTS FOR YOUR JOURNEY

1. List the changes in our culture that have affected the way you live. Which changes do you feel are good and which are harmful? What can you do about the harmful ones?
2. What changes have you experienced in the life of the church? Which do you feel are good and which are harmful? What can you do about the harmful ones?
3. What enables you to cope with change? Are people or books of more help? Is God's Word a source of strength for you in new situations?
4. What is your understanding of conversion after reading this chapter? Think of specific times when you have experienced conversion and have "turned back" to God's ways. Write a prayer of thanksgiving for God's grace.

4 THE LONELY ROAD

[God] gives the lonely a home to live in.
—Psalm 68:6 (TEV)

They confessed that they were strangers and foreigners on the earth.
—Hebrews 11:13

We are for the most part more lonely when we go abroad among men than when we stay in our chambers.
—Henry David Thoreau

The road away from home is often a lonely one. Even the excitement of new vistas and new adventures cannot always compensate for the loneliness of being, like the patriarchs, "strangers and foreigners" in unfamiliar territory.

Throughout the Bible, there are stories of lonely people, traveling down unfamiliar roads, experiencing homesickness, alienation, and homelessness. There's the stark loneliness of Joseph, betrayed by his brothers, a captive in a camel caravan, moving across the desert to a strange land. There's the longing of the Israelites for a homeland as they wandered across the Sinai peninsula. There's Ruth in the "alien corn"; David seeking refuge from the wrath of Saul with the Philistines in Gath; the exiles in Babylon. The psalms of lament touch us deeply because they give expression to the universal human heart cries of the loneliness of alienation, homelessness, grief, and abandonment.

The Gospels make it clear that Jesus himself experienced lonely roads: in the wilderness, where he was tempted; as he traveled through cities and villages in a compassionate effort to meet the overwhelming physical and spiritual needs of the people; as he found he was not accepted by his own people in his own hometown; as he experienced the homelessness of having "nowhere to lay his head"; as he went up the mountain by himself to pray; as he "set his face to go to Jerusalem."

These stories tell us that we are not alone in our loneliness. They remind us that although sometimes God may seem very far away in our lonely times, it is often in these very times that we discover God's presence in a new way. The poet James Weldon Johnson, in his sermon-poem "The Creation," dares to suggest that perhaps there was a time when even God experienced loneliness.[1] If God created human beings in order to ease an unimaginable solitude, as Johnson suggests, then surely God understands our loneliness too.

THE LONELY ROAD OF THE SOJOURNER

The Hebrew word *ger*, which can be translated variously as "sojourner," "stranger," "alien," or even "resident alien," literally means someone who has settled in a strange land and is dependent on the hospitality of the host population. Such people own no land; they have given up the protection of their own tribes or rulers. Abraham, Sarah, and Isaac were described as "strangers and foreigners on the earth" (Heb. 11:13). They were "sojourners" in lands belonging to other people or tribes.

In Old Testament times, the ancient Semitic laws of the desert guaranteed hospitality to strangers. When travelers arrived, hosts were obligated to provide food, shelter, and protection without asking questions. One of the best illustrations of this kind of hospitality is found in the story of Abraham's hospitality to the three men who came to his tent at Mamre (Gen. 18:1–8).[2] Ordinarily, the requirement for hospitality was limited to three days, but sojourners might linger for weeks, months, or even years.

Even when they settled in for a long stay, sojourners were not entitled to own land, but were given permission by the host tribe or king to graze their animals or grow food. Abraham had to get special permission from the Hittites to buy a plot of ground for Sarah's burial place, and succeeded only after a good deal of begging (Gen. 23:4). When sojourners placed themselves under the protection of another individual or tribe, they took on responsibilities of loyalty or fealty to that person or tribe. An example of this is Abraham's relationship to King Abimelech, a relationship that got him into trouble because of his lying to keep the favor of the king (Gen. 20).

The patriarchs were not the only sojourners in the Old Testament. Joseph's brothers came to Egypt as "sojourners," and Pharaoh granted their petition to live in the land of Goshen. David was a sojourner with the Philistines in Gath (ironically, the hometown of Goliath, whom he had slain) when he fled Saul.

The psalms make use of "sojourner" images in powerful ways. In Psalm 39:12, the psalmist cries, "For I am your passing guest, an alien, like all my forebears" and in Psalm 119:19, "I live as an alien in the land; do not hide your commandments from me." These words are a poignant reminder that all human beings are, after all, just "sojourners," enjoying the protection of a host who has extended them hospitality. In Psalm 39, the psalmist is giving us a high and beautiful image of God and God's grace. We are God's guests. We live in God's land. God's generosity sustains us. We exist by God's grace. The answer to the question asked in the first part of the psalm about the meaning of life is found in the phrase "for I am *your* passing guest" (italics added). We are no longer wandering strangers alone in the desert, at the mercy of sand and wind and wild animals. We are guests of the Eternal One, who provides everything we need.

The covenant laws placed great emphasis on the community's responsibility to the sojourner. However, in these laws, sojourners are no longer the Israelites themselves, but the strangers living among them. The laws regarding these sojourners were based on a very important concept found in Exodus 23:9: "You shall not oppress a resident alien; you know the heart of an alien, for you were aliens in the land of Egypt." Israel had known the loneliness and uncertainty that lives in "the heart of an alien," and this covenant law expected them to practice compassion to other sojourners because of that experience. The covenant makes it clear that the same God who saved Israel is also the protector of all the poor, the weak, and the strangers. As God's people, Israel is to provide that same kind of sustenance and protection.

In similar fashion, the New Testament letters strongly remind Christians to express hospitality to strangers (Rom. 12:13; 1 Tim. 3:2; 5:10; Titus 1:8; Heb. 13:2; 1 Pet. 4:9). They were to remember that they, too, were once "aliens from the commonwealth of Israel, and strangers to the covenants of promise" (Eph. 2:12), even though now they are "no longer strangers and aliens," but "citizens with the saints and also members of the household of God" (Eph. 2:19). The Jewish Christians of the Dispersion to whom these letters were written knew what it meant to be sojourners, for even as Jews they had been living as strangers and aliens in a foreign culture. Now, because they had found a new sense of belonging, they were urged to reach out with the simple gift of hospitality to those who felt cut off and alienated.

When science fiction writer Robert Heinlein published his novel, *Stranger in a Strange Land* in the '60s, it became a cult hit with the college-age generation who were a part of the countercultural movement of that decade. Its success was due in part because it tapped into the feeling so frequently expressed by those young people that they no longer felt at home in the world in which they had grown up. They had become alienated from their parents' culture and had become "strangers in a strange land."

This is a hard place to be. Most of us have had a taste of the loneliness of being strangers because of the mobility of our lifestyles. We find ourselves alienated in subdivisions where nobody knows our name or wants to know it. Or when worshiping in unfamiliar churches, where writing one's name in the "Rite of Friendship" book brings no word of greeting from others in the pew, but only a form letter from the pastor. The computer causes increasing insularity and disconnectedness, even from those in the same office. We lapse into a "cubicle mentality," isolating ourselves in our own concerns. Being a stranger means being an outsider, cut off from the easy warmth and familiarity of those who know one another. It's like standing in a cold rain. It's lonely. Thoreau was right when he said that we are for the most part more lonely when we go abroad among others than when we stay home.

In 1989, Stanley Hauerwas and William Willimon wrote a provocative book suggesting that Christians today are "resident aliens" and the church is "an adventurous colony in a society of unbelief,"[3] and they describe the environment:

> A colony is a beachhead, an outpost, an island of one culture in the middle of another, a place where the values of home are reiterated and passed on to the young, a place where the distinctive language and life-style of the resident aliens are lovingly nurtured and reinforced.[4]

Hauerwas and Willimon claim that "to be resident but alien is a formula for loneliness that few of us can sustain" and that the only way we can survive is "by supporting one another through the countless small acts through which we tell one another we are not alone, that God is with us."[5] They argue that the church, as a colony of resident aliens in a post-Christian world, must *be* the church with its own mandate, which is not the mandate of the world around it. They believe that the church's most credible form of witness is "the actual creation of a living, breathing, visible community of faith."[6] More recently, Walter Brueggemann's book *Deep Memory, Exuberant Hope* fleshes out what that community might look like:

> Another world is possible—*in our practice.* . . . Foolishly we enact obedience to a daring claim, obedience to a possibility; we specialize in cold water and shared bread, in welcome speech, hospitality, sharing, giving, compassion, caring, in small ways, setting the world fresh.[7]

We resident aliens, recognizing our strangeness in a post-Christian world, gather together to tell our stories and to pass on our understanding of why it is and how it is we are "different" from the world around us. We resident aliens, in the practice of our faith (bread, water, soup, hugs, tears, hammers, and Band-Aids), demonstrate that difference. We resident aliens do not despise others who are different, but reach out to them in warmth and compassion, in understanding and empathy. We keep God's words in our hearts, recite them to our children, and talk about them when we are at home and when we are away, when we lie down and when we rise (see Deut. 6:6–7). Our loneliness does not go away entirely, but because of these things, our loneliness is bearable. We know that we are sojourners whose lives are undergirded by the grace of the grace-full host.

THE LONELY ROAD OF THE WILDERNESS

After their exodus from Egypt, the Israelites wandered in the wilderness for forty years before entering the promised land. They were not sojourners during this period, for, as Walter Brueggemann suggests, wanderers, in contrast to sojourner-pilgrims, are not on the way to anywhere. Survival is the key question for them.[8] They are not answering a call or responding to a promise, as the patriarchs were, but simply trying to stay alive. This image is in direct contrast to our usual Sunday school picture of the faithful Israelites trudging determinedly through the desert toward their goal: the land of milk and honey. Brueggemann does not deny that they were "dimly on the way," but says that the literature of the wilderness period itself does not indicate that this was a time of resourceful faith. Rather, the mood of the wanderers is bitter, angry, restless, and hopeless.

Many of today's homeless people are just such wanderers in the wilderness. They would recognize Brueggemann's description of the wilderness: "To be placed in the wilderness is to be cast into the land of the enemy—cosmic, natural, historical—without any of the props or resources that give life order and meaning. To be in the wilderness is landlessness par excellence, being not merely a resident alien, as were the fathers, but in a context hostile and destructive."[9] There are striking similarities between that image and this one of contemporary homelessness: "The homeless environment is generally brutal, demoralizing, and stigmatizing. There is increased risk of death, disease, and physical disability for all and of impaired development for children."[10]

In a manual produced for the Presbyterian Church (U.S.A.) on ways to combat homelessness, author Jean Kim comments that "homelessness is rising and spreading like a contagious disease throughout the nation."[11] The grim reality is that families are the fastest-growing segment of the homeless population, accounting for

36 percent of the total nationwide. Millions of Americans have been homeless at some point in their lives.

But homelessness is more than just the lack of a roof over one's head. Homelessness can be emotional and spiritual as well. Emotionally homeless people feel deserted by their families, friends, and even by God. The psalms of lament frequently give expression to this kind of homeless feeling. Psalm 88 is one of these:

> I am like those who have no help,
> like those forsaken among the dead,
>   like the slain that lie in the grave,
> like those whom you remember no more,
>   for they are cut off from your hand.
>   (Ps. 88:4b–5)

The spiritually homeless are those who are searching for meaning and purpose for their lives. Job is the epitome of the spiritually homeless person as he mocks Psalm 8 with his bitter words:

> What are human beings, that you make so much of them,
>   that you set your mind on them,
> visit them every morning,
>   test them every moment?
>   (Job 7:17–18)

What was it that gave the wilderness wanderers hope in their homelessness? What strengthened them to keep going and prevented them from returning to Egypt in spite of their bitter words of longing? The answer is clearly given in Psalm 107, a song that praises the loyal, steadfast love of God (*hesed*), who heard the cries of those who "wandered in desert wastes" (v. 4), and "delivered them from their distress" (v. 6). The psalm declares that God created a highway for those wanderers out of those desert wastes and led them along it. Then the psalmist cries:

Let them thank the LORD for his steadfast love,
    for his wonderful works to humankind.
For he satisfies the thirsty,
    and the hungry he fills with good things.
                                            (Ps. 107:8–9)

James Mays notes that "the psalm teaches the congregation and its members to understand themselves as the redeemed. . . . We are the hungry and thirsty who have been fed. We are the bound who have been liberated. We are the sinners deserving death who have been given life. We are the fearful before the terrors of existence who have been given hope."[12]

When we wander the lonely roads of the wilderness, seeking meaning and purpose for our lives, it is God's steadfast love that sustains us, guides us, and sets our feet on right paths. The psalmist calls us to respond to this love with thanksgiving and praise.

THE EXILES

Exiles are not sojourners. They do not live willingly in another land. They are captives, prisoners of war, deported to a foreign country, and at the mercy of its armies and rulers. The road to exile is a lonely one, full of grief, fear, and despair. We see the faces of those exiles mirrored in the thousands who are displaced from their homes each year. Although not captives, these refugees experience the same combination of terror and loss that the exiles to Babylon felt.

The displacement of populations was a common practice in military conquests of ancient times. Isaiah refers to the exiles in Babylonia poetically as those who had been swallowed up (Isa. 49:19). The deportation of the ten tribes from the northern kingdom had indeed resulted in a "swallowing up." They were assimilated; their identity was lost.

There were three deportations from the southern kingdom to Babylonia between the years 597 and 582 B.C. Because Babylonian policies toward their captives were fairly lenient, many deportees became content upon assimilation, owning their own homes and conducting businesses there, even defecting from the Jewish faith and customs to worship Babylonian gods.

But there were others who never forgot. Their sense of alienation and loneliness and the memories of the homes they had left behind wrapped them like a pall. This longing was powerfully expressed in Psalm 137:

> By the rivers of Babylon—
> there we sat down and there we wept
> when we remembered Zion.
> On the willows there
> we hung up our harps.
> For there our captors
> asked us for songs,
> and our tormentors asked for mirth, saying,
> "Sing us one of the songs of Zion!"
>
> How could we sing the LORD's song
> in a foreign land?
> (Ps. 137:1–4)

The experience of exile is painful and lonely because it means being cut off from one's roots. The familiar patterns, rituals, and friendships that sustain us are no longer there. It is disorienting and calls into question our very being. Although we may never have been to Babylonia, most of us at some point in our lives have to deal with loss, with changes that leave us feeling rootless, and with times of deep loneliness.

My own experience of exile occurred, not in going *to* Africa, but in returning *from* Africa, when my husband began doctoral studies in anthropology at the University of Florida. I had not wanted to leave Africa. My exile was both spiritual and physical. The only place we could afford to rent was twenty miles away from town. The neighbors were not exactly friendly and welcoming. The woman next door explained in her Florida drawl that if I ever wanted to come over, I'd better call first, "because I've got this big dawg . . . and he's a mean 'un." Somehow, this did not come across as an invitation to warm friendship.

To make matters worse, I was alone all day. For the first time, all four of my children (ages 5 to 12) were in school all day. I had no one to talk to about the anger and confusion I felt over my husband's decision to leave the mission field, and the big question that raised about my own call. I felt as if God had abandoned me under those Florida pine trees. I was alone, friendless, and feeling exactly like the despairing person who wrote Psalm 102:

> I am like an owl of the wilderness,
>   like a little owl of the waste places;
> I lie awake,
>   I am like a lonely bird on the housetop.
> . . . .
> For I eat ashes like bread,
>   and mingle tears with my drink, . . .
>   for you have lifted me up and thrown me aside.
> My days are like an evening shadow;
>   I wither away like grass.
>
> (Ps. 102: 6–7, 9–11)

As an outlet for my feelings, I wrote poetry:

> My name is thirty-eight years worn
>   like a smooth stone
>   neither felt nor feeling.
> Its separate syllables speak their cadence
> and I respond with a peculiar little heart-jerk
>   like a puppet on a string.
> But underneath the smoothness
> there's a sea-urchin a-bristle,
>   unseen, untouched, unheard,
>   but weeping to be known.

My loneliness was lessened not only by expressing my feelings in poetry, but by discovering similar pain-filled voices in the psalms of lament like Psalm 137. It was hugely comforting to know that others had walked similar lonesome valleys before me, had also piled covers over their heads, not wanting to face the long, lonely day.

Since then I have learned that the loneliness and distress I felt is not an uncommon experience. The fear of being alone strikes the hearts of many. To be deprived of relationships through the personal "exiles" of change of residence, divorce, or death can be terribly traumatic. Loneliness is about our need for closeness, intimacy, sharing, and nurturance. We don't want to live in exile. We want to belong. We want to be at home.

THE LONELY ROAD TO GETHSEMANE

The Gospels make clear the loneliness of Jesus. After his baptism, he traveled the roads of the wilderness for forty days in a solitary struggle with the tempter. He walked the roads and streets of Galilee with a group of men he had called to be his followers, but they did not always understand him. He was a rabbi trained in the Scriptures, but the scholarly scribes and Pharisees thought him heretical. He spoke of the kingdom of heaven, but the people did not understand. His journey to Jerusalem was a lonely road because of what he knew he had to face. He said to his disciples, "You will all desert me" and Peter's "Never!" was soon replaced by "I do not know the man!"

Jesus' experience in Gethsemane is a paradigm of loneliness. It reveals him as a normal human being, capable of fear, anxiety, and deep despair, his anguished sweat "like great drops of blood falling down on the ground" (Luke 22:44). Clearly, he does not want to drink from the cup of death; he does not have a martyr complex. He wants to do his Father's will, but in some other way than by dying, if possible. He pleads with God, and there is silence. Alone in the depths of the garden, he has to make a heartrendingly difficult decision, without a counselor, pastor, or even a spouse to give him encouragement.

The loneliness of his ordeal is even more painful because his most beloved disciples fail to stand by him in his distress. "Could you not stay awake with me one hour?" (Matt. 26:40), a poignant question that haunts all of us who find our perseverance faltering in spite of our protestations of faithfulness.

Jesus experienced loneliness not because he did not care about people, but because he cared so much: "Come to me, all you that are weary . . . , and I will give you rest" (Matt. 11:28). He experienced loneliness because of his concern that the people were going in wrong directions: "Jerusalem, Jerusalem, the city that kills the prophets and stones those who are sent to it! How often have I desired to gather your children together as a hen gathers her brood under her wings, and you were not willing!" (Matt. 23:37).

Persons of strong faith in the post-Christian world often experience a similar loneliness because they are willing to take risks for their faith:

> Standing for the Christian gospel of compassion for the poor, the stranger, the widows and orphans
>
> Standing by Jesus Christ as Savior and Lord instead of betraying him by unfaithful actions
>
> Standing out in a world given over to manipulation, exploitation, and greed

It's lonely because it means swimming upstream against the secular world's rushing waters. It's lonely because we have a sense of powerlessness and diminished impact in that world. It's lonely because it is difficult to explain to those outside the church just why we are involved in it. It's lonely because the church speaks a language that is no longer a familiar one.

As I reflected on my experience in church life, I realized that often my feeling of loneliness was triggered by excessive workloads I had voluntarily taken on. The result, not uncommon for many in the church today, was exhaustion, exaggerated expectations, and self-pity. I resented that others weren't working as hard as I was, and I would tell myself it was because they didn't care as much. I was lonely on my self-erected pedestal of workaholism.

Sometimes our loneliness comes from the enormity of the task to which we are called as believers: reconciliation. Faithful Christians constantly find themselves in situations where they need to be a reconciling presence: family conflicts, congregational disputes, divisive issues in the life of the larger church. To be a reconciler sounds easy, but it is a lonely task when facing hotly divided opposition. It is a lonely task when one is struggling to find the right words to say. It is a lonely task when one has to speak one's convictions, knowing that some will find them offensive. Above all, it is a bitterly lonely task when one's efforts at reconciliation have failed. Jesus knew this bitter loneliness. Paul knew it as well, and yet he could write: "If . . . there is any encouragement in Christ, any consolation from love, any sharing in the Spirit, any compassion and sympathy, make my joy complete: be of the same mind, having the same love, being in full accord and of one mind" (Phil. 2:1).

THE LONELY ROAD TO BETHANY

When I was a teenager, everyone in our church youth group knew John 11:35. We knew it because in the customary translations it was the shortest verse in the Bible, and therefore was the easiest one to remember when we were called on to recite a Bible verse. Most of us had never been to the funeral of a friend—there were no school shootings in those innocent days—and so we failed to grasp the terrible poignancy of those two brief words: "Jesus wept."

He wept as he was on a road, the road to Bethany, the place of his solace and comfort. That road had been transformed into a lonely road of grief by the news of Lazarus's death. "See how he loved him!" observers said. His tears spoke eloquently of the grief that possessed him.

Why is the loneliness of grief so painful? Perhaps it is because underlying our grief is the fear of the emotionally homeless: the feeling of abandonment, the feeling that no one knows we exist, that no one cares, not even God.

Several years ago, I asked the women at a retreat to write one line describing the word "loneliness." Their responses frequently were dominated by images of grief and abandonment:

Loneliness is being trapped inside a pit, shouting to God, but no one answers.

Loneliness is being a motherless child. You left me before I ever knew you.

Loneliness is losing the daily embrace, the outlet for sharing, the reason for coming home.

Loneliness is wandering lost in the woods, driving down a highway that has no direction signs.

Loneliness is a dark room with no windows or doors, where my soul feels forgotten and lost.

Loneliness is talking and no one is there.

These poignant expressions are the heart cries of those who have traveled the lonely road of grief. They have lost spouses, children, parents, and friends. They have walked through the dark valleys of illness and death, loss and rejection. They have felt, oftentimes, abandoned by the God they love and want to serve. They cry out, "Why, O Lord?"

The story of Jesus in Gethsemane gives us a model for coping with and understanding our own lonely hours of abandonment, grief, and despair. Even when abandoned by his friends and rejected by his own people, Jesus refused to abandon the will of God. Strengthened by earnest, unflinching prayer, he was finally able to say from the bottom of his heart, "Not what I want, but what you want" (Matt. 26:39). Obedience does not come easily when we are afraid and lonely. Rebellion does. It is easy to cry out like Job, "I cry to you and you do not answer me; I stand, and you merely look at me. You have turned cruel to me" (Job 30:20–21a). Jesus gives us a more difficult model of acceptance and obedience. We are not to give in to despair, but we are to say with Christ, "See, God, I have come to do your will" (Heb. 10:7). The Gethsemane story reminds us that when our road is lonely, someone who understands that loneliness walks that road with us.

THE LONELY ROAD TO CALVARY

The worst sense of abandonment is feeling abandoned by God. Even in Gethsemane, Jesus never hints that he felt abandoned by God, as he was by his friends. Mark's version of the story tells us that in Gethsemane Jesus addressed God with the loving, affectionate term "Abba," which can be translated "Daddy." It was not until he hung from the cross that he shouted those tragic words from Psalm 22: "My God, my God, why have you forsaken me?" These stark words raise the question: Did Jesus really feel abandoned by God? Biblical scholar Douglas R. A. Hare explains: "Matthew believes that he did and retains the troubling question because it points to the deepest mystery of the saving event. . . . If Jesus is abandoned by God, it can only be because he is giving his life as a ransom for sinners. Separation from God is the price of sin."[13]

The theme of abandonment is a common one in the psalms. Nearly half of the psalms are songs of lament, and many of these begin with lines like these, from Psalm 13: "How long, O Lord? Will you forget me forever? How long will you hide your face from me?" When poet Ann Weems's twenty-one-year-old son was killed, she drew on the pattern of these lament psalms to give voice to her grief. Her psalms were published under the title *Psalms of Lament*. She describes in one her sense of abandonment:

> O God, I live in the land of the forgotten,
> I stretch out my hand to you,
> and there is nothing.
> I cry night and day,
> and you do not take pity on me.
> I pray to you,
> but you turn away.
> O God, why won't you help me?[14]

Every month I lead a Bible study for a small group of women. All except two are widows. Three have lost sons in their thirties and forties, one of them a suicide. One woman has buried a husband and four sons. One woman has a brain tumor;

one is a cancer survivor. Our study of Job and the lament psalms was not a dry academic exercise. The women were able to share their feelings of being abandoned by God in these terrible crises. One admitted, "I wanted to be angry at God and cry out, but I kept it all inside." Our study of Job and Psalms helped them understand that to give voice to pain, loss, and even anger is an appropriate form of prayer.

The psalms do not leave us in a dark room with no windows. The testimony of the psalms is that the darkness can be dispelled, the gloom of the pit of loneliness dispersed. Psalm 18:28 offers this shining hope: "It is you who light my lamp; the LORD, my God, lights up my darkness." Even Psalm 22, with its bleak opening words, concludes with a message of affirmation:

> For he did not despise or abhor
>   the affliction of the afflicted;
> he did not hide his face from me,
>   but heard when I cried to him.
>   (Ps. 22:24)

If we can embrace our loneliness, we will find its healing power. We will find that God is just as present to us in our loneliness as in our joy. When Jesus felt alone in the garden and cried out to his father, he received the protection of a parent's presence. We are not alone. Christ understands our suffering, our alienation, our lostness. He walks the lonely roads with us.

LONELINESS AND COMMUNITY

Most of us have deep wells of loneliness inside us. Just before I was to begin the seventh grade, my family moved to a small town and I entered a school where it seemed as if everybody knew everybody—except for me. The others in my class had been together since the first grade. I was a stranger, an outsider, and it didn't feel a bit good. I still dream about the loneliness of those days.

Our journeys are not meant to be utterly solitary. We need others to walk those lonely roads with us. Often, however, we are like shy seventh-graders. We would like to share our lives with others, to feel connected and known, but something gets in the way. The more cut off from intimate sharing we are, the more acute our loneliness.

We need to stay aware of two barriers to sharing. One barrier is the feeling of inferiority. This feeling is, more often than not, self-inflicted. It makes us fearful of sharing. What do I have to offer another? How will the other respond? I'll be embarrassed. She will cut me off. So we allow our fears to shield us from the risk of sharing in relationships. And we grow lonelier still.

The other barrier is almost the opposite. We are not willing to acknowledge that we can't make it on our own. Yet if we are to have close relationships, it is essential that we admit to our need and be willing to receive what another has to offer. All the teaching we have received mitigates against this. We are supposed to be self-sufficient, or at least to appear so. We live in an age when individualism and independence are perceived as marks of strength. To admit hurt or need or loneliness is considered a sign of weakness. Under no circumstances are we to let others see our vulnerability.

Jesus' life gives us another model to follow. He was not hesitant about taking on the risks of intimate relationships. He called a group of twelve men to be with him as disciples and companions. He traveled the road to Bethany on more than one occasion to seek the company of his friends Mary, Martha, and Lazarus. He was not afraid to be vulnerable. He shared with his disciples his dark premonitions of pain and death. He spoke candidly and openly of his love for them. He made it clear that he needed their friendship, support, and loyalty. If Jesus needed others, how much more do we?

In my time of exile after returning from the Congo, my bruised spirit went into hibernation. For four months, I did not participate in the life of a faith community. I felt that I could not face all those bright, happy, sunshiny Christians. I put up the first barrier, saying to myself, I have nothing to give to anyone else, because I am so spiritually drained. Besides, what would they think of a missionary who has left her vocation? And then I added the second: I don't need the church. I can get along very well by myself.

I was wrong, of course, on both counts. At the end of those bleak four months, I experienced a desperate longing for community, and I went to church again. The community of sisters and brothers I found ministered to me, even without knowing the depth of my depression. They accepted me the way I was, and helped set me on my feet again. The road became less lonely because I had found traveling companions who helped me over the rocky places and pointed me in the right direction. Little by little, joy began to return to my life, and meaning, and a sense of purpose. The impact of that community has been long-lasting. The road has never been as lonely since.

Something else happened in that small community of faithful people. Grace Church was well named, for through the *grace* of worship, the *grace* I experienced in the lives of the people, and the *grace* of God's love, I came to realize that I had never really been alone. I renewed my commitment to the One who had been my companion all along, even when I was unaware of his presence, the One who had traveled lonely roads himself. When the dark night had descended, he was there beside me. When I was aching to be known, he knew me by heart. When I had no sense of purpose, he was whispering (if only I had listened), "Just you wait!"

CONCLUSION

We keep trying to go it alone. But when we do, the loneliness looms larger and blacker. We need companions who will walk our lonely roads with us. And we need Christ, the Christ of Gethsemane, the agonized Christ on the cross, who knows and understands the depths of our alienation, our grief, our loneliness. He says to us, "Peace I leave with you; my peace I give to you. I do not give to you as the world gives. Do not let your hearts be troubled, and do not let them be afraid" (John 14:27).

GUIDEPOSTS FOR YOUR JOURNEY

1. Write a one-line poetic definition of loneliness. If you are in a group, collect the definitions and redistribute them to group members. Ask each person to write a lament psalm addressing the loneliness expressed in the definition they have received. Read these psalms aloud.

2. If you would like to know more about what your church can do about homelessness, order *"End Homelessness," a jubilee manual,* by Jean Kim. It includes a description of successful program models used by churches, along with worship resources. The cost is $10, and it can be ordered from Presbyterian Distribution Services (1-800-524-2612).

3. Reach out to a person who is lonely today. If you don't know such a person, be especially attentive as you go about your daily routines. The chances are good that you will find one.

4. Memorize some Scripture to carry you through the dark times. Some suggestions:

"Father of orphans and protector of widows is God in his holy habitation. God gives the desolate a home to live in." (Ps. 68:5–6)

"I will not leave you orphaned; I am coming to you." (John 14:18)

"Remember, I am with you always." (Matt. 28:20)

"It is the LORD who goes before you. He will be with you; he will not fail you or forsake you. Do not fear or be dismayed." (Deut. 31:8)

5   AT THE CROSSROADS

Stand at the crossroads, and look,
    and ask for the ancient paths,
where the good way lies; and walk in it,
    and find rest for your souls.
                       Jeremiah 6:16

The most difficult choices in life are not between the good and the evil, but between the good and the best.

                       G. B. Caird

The road goes ever on and on . . . until it finds some larger way
Where many paths and errands meet.
                       J. R. R. Tolkien

It always happens. Just when everything is going well and we are proceeding serenely down the road of life, we come to a crossroads and have to make choices. A job opportunity arises. We meet a special someone. A spouse dies. The economy falters and we find ourselves out of work. A call comes from God to a new vocation.

Life would be so much easier if it would just let us be and not keep pushing us to make choices. Think how easy robots have it. Their behavior is programmed, and they never have the stress of making choices. As for us, every time we come to one of life's crossroads we agonize and nail-bite and drive our family members crazy trying to decide what to do. I love new challenges, but they scare me to death. Every time I have had to make a choice to launch out into something new, I find myself saying, "I know I can't do it! I'm just not up to it!" On one occasion, after hearing that very comment, my daughter sighed and said, "Oh, Mom, you always say that!" The truth is, I really am more comfortable being tentative, moving in cautious hesitancies, than in taking risks and making bold choices. I'd rather shrink back into my cocoon than be a butterfly. I'd rather hide in the nest than try to soar.

I'm not the only person who has suffered the agony of crossroads. One of the most famous pieces ever written about choice making is Robert Frost's poem, "The Road Not Taken," in which the poet describes making a hard choice between two roads and the difference that choice made in his life.

The trouble is that life's really big choices are difficult even when we get lots of good advice from family and friends, even when we read all the right "Seven Steps" books, even when we think we know what we want. All of us have faced serious times of choice making in our lives involving the kind of decisions that have, as Frost said, "made all the difference," affecting who we are and what we have become.

The Bible is the story of choices made at various crossroads by God's people, and the theological implications of those choices. Although the word "crossroads" is used only twice in the NRSV, in Proverbs 8:2 and Jeremiah 6:16, there are many crossroads experiences where biblical characters had to make crucial decisions about which way to go. Reflecting on these moments of decision making provides us with patterns for discovering "where the good way lies" when we face our own crossroads.

CROSSROADS IN CANAAN: PERSEVERANCE VS. GIVING UP

I once knew a young girl who had the gift of coining phrases that became mantras for the rest of her group of friends. One of her phrases has stayed with me through the years: Perseverance will pull you through! As I think about Abraham and Sarah answering God's call to leave Haran and venture into Canaan, I find that phrase extremely apt. It took a lot of perseverance for them to remain faithful to the promise they had received. Hebrews 11 says, "By faith Abraham . . . set out, not knowing where he was going . . . stayed for a time in the land . . . died . . . without having received the promises" (vv. 8, 9, 13). That's perseverance! They could have turned back, "if they had been thinking of the land that they had left behind" (Heb. 11:15).

There were no clearly marked crossroads for Abraham and Sarah in their migratory life, but they still had to make choices. As they huddled in goatskin tents, watching the desert sandstorms hurtling around them, they must have been constantly tempted to turn back and give up their pilgrimage. They had to decide whether to live for the promise of God or to live against it. This is not an easy thing to do, because, as Walter Brueggemann says, "faith in God's promise is a possibility which the world sees as scandalous."[1] The world argues for behavior that stands in opposition to God's promises: Don't be different—be just like everybody else! Get ahead at all costs! Go for the good life; you deserve it!

The sad reality is that Abraham and Sarah did not always make the right choices. They sometimes yielded to the world's voices, rather than remaining faithful to the promises of God. Abraham lied about Sarah's being his sister, to save his skin in Egypt. Sarah sent Hagar to Abraham when her faith in God's outrageous promise of an heir grew thin. We can understand their failures, for they are ours. All too often our own decisions at crossroads resemble those faithless responses of Abraham and Sarah. We make our decisions out of fear or lack of faith, or conformity to the world's ways, or just to have "the good life."

In spite of all their lapses, however, Abraham and Sarah are held up in the Letter to the Hebrews as examples of those who knew some secrets about being faithful followers of God. What was it that kept them focused in spite of their falterings? What kept them from giving up and turning back? What can we learn from their faithful continuance? Preacher and teacher Thomas G. Long sees Abraham and Sarah's journey of faith as possessing many of the characteristics of all faith journeys, and cites these three in particular:

They had a deep trust in the One who was sending them.

They recognized that they were utterly dependent on God for provisions along the way.

Their destination was never in doubt.[2]

These qualities acted like compasses to help them make the right choices, and they can serve as compasses for us in our own times of decision making.

Trusting in God is not always easy. We are besieged with questions as we face directions and choices in our journeys. Will I be hurt? Is it dangerous? What will happen to me? It takes faith to have enough trust to turn ourselves completely over into the hands of God and follow God wherever God leads us. Trusting God does not mean having all the answers. It does mean believing in God's steadfast love. The Hebrew word translated as "steadfast love" is *hesed*, one of the most marvelous words in the Hebrew Bible. It means "unshakable covenantal love," the kind God expresses in the statement "I . . . will be your God, and you shall be my people." God is faithful even when we are not.

We give a lot of lip service to dependence on God for our provisions, but the reality is that stock market unreliability creates a lot of anxiety in a lot of Christian hearts. Do we really believe that God will provide? Or do we secretly think that is just a pious platitude not to be counted on? Most of us walk the road of life under a cloud of worry, doubting God's provisions, but when we are able to move forward in obedience and trust, we find God does not fail us. Our God is the God who provides manna in the wilderness, honey in the rock, and oases in the desert of parched places. Our God gives us the perseverance to pull us through.

I don't think I fully grasped this until 1960, when my husband and I lost everything we owned. When independence came like a bolt of lightning to the Congo, we found ourselves homeless refugees with nothing except the clothes on our back, a bag of diapers, and two little boys, ages two and four. We had no place to go. Our home, our belongings, our job had disappeared overnight. But God did provide. Through the help of family, friends, and the church we were sheltered, fed, and cared for. It was a lesson I shall never forget: that even in the most difficult situations, trusting in God's steadfast love provides a compass that guides and directs our path.

Abraham and Sarah knew where they were going. The words in Hebrews 11:15 are so poignant: "If they had been thinking of the land that they had left behind. . . ." If all their meaning had lain in the past, if they were energized by nostalgia instead of adventure, then they might as well have turned back. But they didn't give in to home-sickness, or to a false romanticizing of the past that would have left them immobilized, moaning, "If only things were the way they used to be." That kind of romanticizing is a hobby in some churches. People talk about the good old days when the church was small and everybody knew everybody, or when the church was large and there were a lot of young people. It's also common in our own lives. We think wistfully about the lands we have left behind and wonder why life has never been as good since high school, or since the children were young, or since we had a career. We spend so much time living in our photo albums and scrapbooks that the world around us goes by unnoticed, and we forget about the homeland we should be actively seeking.

Our dreams don't always get realized in the way we plan. Abraham and Sarah never got to that city whose architect and builder is God, but greeted it from afar, as Hebrews says. They died without having received the fulfillment of all God's promises. They perished without completing the pilgrimage, but they never lost hope. They kept focused on God's steadfast love. They were on a forward-looking journey. They were in search of a better country. When they came to crossroads, they remained faithful to the promise that had been given them, and because of that faith, Scripture says, God is not ashamed to be called their God. What more beautiful tribute could there be?

CROSSROADS AT THE JORDAN: LIFE VS. DEATH

A few years ago, I rediscovered the book of Deuteronomy. My guide for this rediscovery was Patrick D. Miller's volume in the Interpretation Bible Commentary series, published by John Knox Press. I had never before realized how central this book is to the Hebrew Bible, and how important a knowledge of it is for a proper understanding of the New Testament. The book is presented as Moses' words to all

Israel before they entered the land that God had promised, and it was meant, Miller says, "to found a people and to guide their ongoing life."[3]

Israel had reached a crossroads, both geographically and spiritually. The people were in Moab, poised to cross the Jordan River into the promised land. It was a time for decision making about allegiances. Would they fear "this glorious and awesome name, the LORD your God" (Deut. 28:58) or would they "serve other gods, of wood and stone" (28:36)? In Deuteronomy 29, God instructs Moses to call the people to a renewal of the covenant vows they had taken at Sinai. In the first part of Deuteronomy, Moses had wasted no words reminding the people of their faithlessness to that covenant: "You rebelled", "you grumbled", "you have no trust in the LORD your God." He had also reminded them of the wondrous truth of God's faithfulness: "These forty years the LORD your God has been with you; you have lacked nothing" (2:7). It is because of the people's unfaithfulness, and God's faithfulness, that this renewed commitment is necessary.

Deuteronomy 29 and 30 spell out the meaning of the covenant. The people are to show their obedience "by observing his commandments and decrees that are written in this book of the law," and by turning to the Lord "with all your heart and with all your soul." These words echo the Shema of Deuteronomy 6:4, identified by Jesus as "the greatest and first commandment." The laws in Deuteronomy are the instruction manual for how the people are to live in the land of promise. Obedience to them is not to be taken lightly. It is a matter of "life and prosperity" or "death and adversity." Which will it be, blessings or curses? Moses asks. Then he urges, "Choose life so that you and your descendants may live, loving the LORD your God, obeying him, and holding fast to him" (30:19). Miller says, "That commitment is what the covenant is about and what Deuteronomy is about."[4] This moment of decision, of choice making, forms the book's dramatic climax. Miller summarizes:

> To live in the land according to the directions given about all these things in the Torah of the Lord, God's instruction, is to create the possibilities for a good and blessed life. To live in some other way, however, is to choose the way of death and catastrophe.[5]

I do not remember when I made my first decision to choose life, but I do know that I have had to make that decision over and over again, as new crossroads appear. Those alternative highways can look as inviting as German autobahns, or as innocent as a winding country road in the spring, and still be avenues to death. As Frost said, the roads we choose "[make] all the difference" in the blessings or curses life offers us. When we arrive at life's crossroads, it is a time for us too to make a renewed commitment to the covenant we have made with our God.

That commitment includes a renewed commitment to the instructions God has given us in how life should be lived. It may seem trite or easy to say, "Read the Bible," when you face serious decisions, but the rule of Occam's razor says that the simplest solution is preferable. In this day of serious biblical illiteracy, we turn to every other quick-fix source of advice we can find, but ignore the Good Book. Deuteronomy makes a strong case for the importance of knowing God's Word, keeping it in our hearts, reciting it to our children, talking about it at home and away from home, on going to bed and on getting up in the morning. If we were to do this, we would have a stronger picture of which way might be God's way when we stand at the crossroads.

In spite of all the emphasis on choice, however, any talk of covenant must recognize that the choosing was first done by God. One cannot read through Deuteronomy without noticing how often the phrase "God chose" appears. The people had already been chosen out of God's loving-kindness *(hesed)*. Now it was their turn, in the covenant contract, to choose to respond to that *hesed* by choosing to love, obey, and hold fast to God. We choose the God who chooses us. "We love because he first loved us" (1 John 4:19).

CROSSROADS IN MOAB AND BETHLEHEM: *HESED* VS. SELF-CONCERN

The story of Ruth is one of the most well-known and well-loved short stories in the Old Testament. Ruth's famous words to Naomi, "Whither thou goest, I will go" (Ruth 1:16 KJV), have been sung or recited at countless weddings. The poignant figure of Ruth, standing "amid the alien corn," as Keats described her, has also been portrayed in literature by such figures as Victor Hugo, Irving Fineman, and Jessamyn West. Her story is one of family loyalty and fidelity, but it is also more than that. It is a story of caring and responsibility for others. It is a story that provides a moving illustration of the word *hesed*. While this complex term is usually used to speak of God's steadfast love, Old Testament scholar Katherine Sakenfeld provides a fresh perspective on its meaning:

> The Hebrew term *(hesed)* is a strong one. It refers to care or concern for another with whom one is in relationship, but care that specifically takes shape in action to rescue the other from a situation of desperate need, and under circumstances in which the rescuer is uniquely qualified to do what is needed.[6]

Sakenfeld then lists examples of *hesed* that are found in the book of Ruth:

> Ruth's determination to accompany Naomi on the journey from Moab to Bethlehem
>
> Ruth's continuing care in seeking food for the despairing Naomi and her willingness to cooperate in the risky visit to the threshing floor
>
> Boaz's special provision for Ruth to glean
>
> Boaz's ready agreement to pursue the arrangement for the marriage
>
> Naomi's offering a plan for the security and happiness of her daughters-in-law
>
> Naomi's initiating a new plan for Ruth's future[7]

Note that it is not just Ruth who expresses concern for others; Naomi, Boaz, and the men and women of Bethlehem also show *hesed*.

The story begins in Moab, the same territory east of the Dead Sea where Moses gave his farewell "life or death" address. Naomi, Orpah, and Ruth had reached a crossroads in their lives. Their husbands had all died, and they were faced with a critical decision about their future. Naomi and her husband, Elimelech, had gone to

Moab because of famine in their hometown, Bethlehem. Word had come that the famine was now over, because "the LORD had . . . given them food." The three women set out for Bethlehem. We are not told how far they went together before they came to a symbolic "crossroads," a moment for decision. "Go back," Naomi urges the two women. "Go back to your mother's house. Go back and marry again and find security."

Again, I am indebted to Katherine Sakenfeld for pointing out how Naomi's blessing incorporates the three main criteria of an act of *hesed*:

1. The action is essential to the survival or basic well-being of the recipient.
2. The action is one that only the person doing the act of *hesed* is in a position to provide.
3. The action is requested within the context of an existing, established, and positive relationship. It does not refer to actions where forgiveness is needed to reestablish a positive relationship, i.e., it is not the same as "grace."[8]

Naomi commits Orpah and Ruth to God's *hesed* and at the same time sets them free from any commitment to her. Orpah does the proper thing and takes her mother-in-law's advice to take the road home. She is not to be faulted for this, but her decision to obey convention and settle for known security makes what Ruth does all the more extraordinary. At this crossroads in her life, Ruth chooses the road into a strange land. She chooses to leave behind all that is familiar for a new life and new loyalties. There are echoes of Abraham and Sarah's decision here, except there is no hint of a "call." Ruth's choice of a road is dictated by her love for Naomi and her loyalty to her.

In her promise to Naomi, Ruth makes a commitment not only to offer companionship and support, but to be a part of her community and to worship her God. It is a lifelong commitment. She will die where Naomi dies and will be buried with her. This is a truly remarkable commitment, for in biblical days burial in one's homeland was considered extremely important.[9]

It is no wonder that this amazing statement of commitment has moved people through the centuries. And it is no wonder that Ruth's words have come to symbolize the kind of family relationships for which we yearn. We would like our families to be ones where an atmosphere of basic acceptance, caring, and respect makes it possible for family members to weather their differences. Is it too much to expect families in the community of faith to live according to the rules of *hesed*? One of the first verses I learned in Sunday school was "Be ye kind one to another, tenderhearted, forgiving one another" (Eph. 4:32 KJV). It's good advice for families to remember. We need to set a priority on loving those around us. We need to learn to express our feelings of affection and warmth, of concern and caring. Anger and criticism are even more painful and hurtful when they are the only exchanges between family members. Ruth's love for Naomi was so evident that the women of Bethlehem described her as "your daughter-in-law who loves you, who is more to you than seven sons." They are referring to Ruth's *hesed*, her faithfulness, kindness, and loyalty to Naomi.[10]

When Ruth came to a crossroads in her personal life, she made a decision for *hesed*. We face many crossroads in our own personal lives: our decisions to marry, to have children, to divorce, to let our children go, to keep our children bound to us, to take full responsibility for aging parents or to place them in nursing homes. Unfortunately our decision making is not always rooted and grounded in *hesed*. All too often, it is based on a "What's in it for me?" attitude. When we approach decision making with that mind-set, we are frequently disillusioned with the results: "It just didn't work out." "I can't do a thing with that kid!" "My parents expect too much from me."

When we come to crossroads in our relationships, our decisions will make a difference in whether those relationships are to be destructive or nourishing, healthy or crippling. Choosing the path of *hesed* will "[make] all the difference."

CROSSROADS ON THE ROAD TO JERUSALEM: DETERMINATION VS. HESITANCY

The Gospel of Luke puts special emphasis on the importance of Jesus' last journey to Jerusalem. This journey has similarities to the exodus, the wilderness wanderings, and the entry into the promised land. His exodus was from his home territory of Galilee. His wilderness wanderings were, according to Matthew 19:1, in "the region of Judea beyond the Jordan," and the promised land was Jerusalem, the Holy City, the place where the Messiah would reign.

Jesus' journey begins with a phrase that indicates an important crossroads marker in his life: "he set his face to go to Jerusalem." These words recall Isaiah's description of the Suffering Servant: "I have set my face like flint, and I know that I shall not be put to shame; he who vindicates me is near" (Isa. 50:7–8). The phrase "he set his face" gives a clear indication of the determination with which Jesus made his decision at this definitive crossroads in his life and ministry. He chose the road to Jerusalem with a sense of commitment to his destiny as a "suffering servant." His awareness of that destiny colors everything that happens to him along that road. He does not seem to hesitate or to want to run away from what he knows lies ahead. There is no agonized pleading with God as occurs later in Gethsemane. Instead, he "set his face" and went calmly on his chosen way.

The road Jesus chose was not a straight line from Galilee to Jerusalem. Although his route cannot be precisely traced, Matthew tells us he crossed over the Jordan into the region known as Perea, part of the kingdom (along with Galilee) ruled by Herod Antipas. Why did he choose this circuitous route instead of going directly south? The reason is indicated in Luke 9:52–56. By Jesus' time, there was extreme tension and hostility between the Jews and the Samaritans. The age-old race war that had begun over the "mixed blood" of the Samaritans had escalated into distinct divisions. The Samaritans had their own place of worship and accepted only the Pentateuch as Scripture. They despised the pilgrims to Jerusalem who passed through their territory, were often openly hostile to them, refusing food and hospitality. When Jesus sent disciples ahead to make arrangements for food and shelter, they were refused and were forced to take another route.

The road Jesus took through Perea was frequently traveled by Galilean pilgrims to Jerusalem in order to avoid encountering Samaritans. Jesus did not move through Perea quickly (Luke gives his journey nearly nine chapters: 9:51–18:34), but remained for some time, continuing his ministry of healing and teaching.

Luke's description of the journey to Jerusalem contains a distinct emphasis on Jesus' teaching about decision making. There is a similarity between this journey and the book of Deuteronomy. Just as Deuteronomy was a guide for devout Jews, presented as a journey to the promised land, so Luke offers a handbook on discipleship in the setting of a journey to Jerusalem.[11]

In contrast to Jesus' determination is the wavering uncertainty of three potential followers of Jesus, described in Luke 9:57–62. These three were also at a crossroads time of decision making. The first is a volunteer, bursting with eagerness to travel the road with Jesus, until Jesus reminds him that the road of discipleship may call for the loss of personal security and independence. The second person seems ready and willing to answer Jesus' invitation, but first makes a logical request: to take care of his responsibilities in the death of his father. Jesus suggests that even these important filial duties take second place to the proclamation of the kingdom. The third person is also eager to follow Jesus, but asks permission to say good-bye to loved ones. Jesus' answer—no hesitation allowed if you are to be worthy of the kingdom—seems almost unduly harsh.

The strange thing about this passage is that all three of these people have very good reasons for delaying their acceptance of Jesus' invitation. We have often used similar excuses for postponing our own good intentions about answering God's call to us. The point of the passage is simple: Jesus' call is to radical discipleship. To follow him means much more than to walk casually along beside him on a journey. In his commentary on Luke, Fred Craddock says this story reminds us that "the radicality of Jesus' words lies in his claim to priority over the best, not the worst, of human relationships."[12] This crossroads decision is not an easy one; in fact, it may be the most difficult one to make for those who would follow Jesus. It shows us clearly what Jesus meant when he said, "Take up [your] cross and follow me." That cross is not always physical punishment. It may be the agonizing decision making between "the good" and "the best."

The uncertainty these three people felt is also demonstrated by another person who had to make a crossroads decision after his encounter with Jesus. He is described variously as "a certain ruler" (Luke 18:18), a "young man" (Matt. 19:20), and simply as "a man" (Mark 10:17). All three Gospels say he was rich, so we know him as "the rich young ruler." Mark tells us Jesus loved him. He seems to be a serious seeker. At least he asks a serious question: "What good must I do to have eternal life?" This is the characteristic question of those who have bought into the idea of salvation by works or "works righteousness." It is not uncommon among good church people today. Perhaps the young man wanted some corroboration of his "righteous" lifestyle, but instead of providing that, Jesus gave him five commands: Go, sell, give, come, follow. Once more, he defined the seriousness of discipleship. Once more, he brought someone to a crossroads of decision making. And the young man wavered. He was shocked. He was sad. He couldn't bring himself to say yes to these demands. He was paralyzed by the choice before him. Unable to choose Jesus' way, he "went away grieving." He finally made a choice at this crossroads, but it was not for the one who loved him. "The entry of any man into eternal life or into the kingdom is a miracle of God's grace, which cannot be earned but only accepted with humility and faith. The peril of possessions is that they stand in the way of this receptive faith."[13]

As if these stories about determination and wavering were not enough, Luke and Matthew include in the journey to Jerusalem instructions for discipleship that have a strong emphasis on crossroads decision making. In Matthew these instructions are given to the Twelve, but in Luke they are spoken to the "large crowds" that had joined Jesus and the Twelve and were traveling the road to Jerusalem with him.

I was in Beijing on May 17, 1989, the day after an estimated one million demonstrators filled Tiananmen Square in support of freedom. As our bus proceeded toward the square, we had to come to a complete stop. The streets were filled with hundreds of Chinese, mostly young people, making their way to join the others in the square on foot, on bicycle, on mopeds, and in cars and trucks. There was a festive air—smiling faces, singing, waving friendly greetings, flashing V for victory signs to those of us on the bus. The demonstrators were caught up in the joyous anticipation of victory. They had no idea of the reality of the sacrifice they would be making, that in less than two weeks army tanks would move into that square, and many of them would lose their lives or be imprisoned for inciting rebellion.

Were the crowds following Jesus similar to those enthusiastic youth? Were they anticipating a victory in Jerusalem? Were they marching along with a festive air? Jesus seems to think so, for he stops, turns around to them, and gives it to them straight: Hate your families, hate your life, carry the cross. The word "hate" as it is used here does not mean dislike, but detachment. Jesus is saying that the claims of the gospel take precedence over all other claims: families, communities, governments, even the preciousness of life itself. He is confronting the crowds with a major crossroads decision and some serious questions about it: "Have you counted the cost? Do you know what you are doing? Have you got the determination to see it through?" Salt can lose its saltiness, he says. Discipleship can lose its faith and fervor. Jesus is calling the crowd to crossroads decision making, to a serious, realistic, wholehearted commitment.

Brother Roger of the Taizé Community in France wrote these eloquent words about the decision to which Jesus calls us:

> He confronts us with an alternative: "Whoever would save their life will lose it. Whoever gives their life for love of me will find it." But Christ does not impose the choice. He leaves each one free to choose him or to reject him. He never forces us. Simple, gentle, and humble of heart, he has been standing for two thousand years at the door of every human heart and knocking: "Do you love me?"[14]

GIFTS AT THE CROSSROADS

The only two passages in the NRSV that make explicit references to crossroads offer poetic glimpses of the gifts and opportunities offered by crossroads.

Proverbs 8:2: The Gifts of Wisdom

The crossroads passage in Proverbs 8:2 is part of a poem that personifies Wisdom as a woman calling to young people. In Proverbs, wisdom is both an attribute of God and a virtue to be sought, possessed, and embraced by students and sages.[15] There are six important elements of wisdom in ancient Israel: knowledge, imagination, discipline, piety, order, and moral instruction.[16] Of these, Proverbs 8 emphasizes moral instruction and presents Wisdom as a teacher who invites people to come and learn. She is offering courses in prudence, intelligence, righteousness, and truth. She is not offering these courses in a classroom, but "on the heights," "beside the way," "at the crossroads," and "beside the gates in the front of the town." This would not have been at all unusual in ancient Israel. Gates served as civic centers, as marketplaces, as news centers, and even as courts, where the elders of the city sat to act as judges in legal matters (see Deut. 21:19 and Ruth 4:1). It was at the city gates that Absalom did his politicking in his plot to usurp his father's throne, and "stole the hearts of the people of Israel" (see 2 Sam. 15:2–6). Because of all of this legal and commercial activity, the city gates, and the roads that led up to them, were places where itinerant teachers often gathered to instruct their students.

In Proverbs 8, wisdom is found in the midst of the hustle and bustle of life, not just in the silent meditation of the contemplative life. It is precisely in the middle of the realities of daily existence that wisdom provides instruction for how life is to be lived. This instruction offers the means by which we can live in harmony with the world and experience success in all our daily pursuits, from business to family to politics. At the crossroads of life we have the opportunity to learn prudence, intelligence, noble things, and "what is right" (Prov. 8:5–6).

It is fascinating to look at these four terms from the standpoint of road imagery.

> *Prudence.* In Wisdom literature, the word for prudence, *ormah,* is always used in the sense of shrewdness, or the ability to keep oneself from being misled, an important skill for persons at crossroads. Often we learn prudence by trial and error. When we do take wrong roads, those bad decisions may prevent us from making the same mistakes again. "We got lost trying to find your house," friends of ours said, "we took a wrong turn at the crossroads." They learned prudence through that mistake, and won't be misled next time.
>
> *Intelligence or understanding.* The root meaning of *bin,* the Hebrew word usually translated as "to understand," is "to divide or to separate," so "understanding" really means the ability to distinguish between right and wrong.

This is the critical choice at crossroads. Which road is the right direction to take and which is wrong? The first chapters of Proverbs put much emphasis on the importance of taking the right paths (see Prov. 2:9 and 3:6) and avoiding the wrong ones (see Prov. 1:15 and 2:18, 19).

Noble things. The Hebrew word translated as "noble things" in the NRSV literally means "princes." Some translators feel this is a scribal error, and want to substitute a similar Hebrew word which means "true things." However, because the text returns to a mention of princes and nobles in verse 15, "By me princes rule, and nobles govern the earth" (RSV), there seems to be justification for keeping the translation of "noble" or "princely." Rulers must make decisions for the good of the community. Good government can be achieved only when rulers follow the way of wisdom, when they choose the right roads. Similarly, our decisions affect the lives of others as well as our own. At our crossroads, we need noble wisdom, the kind good rulers have, as we make those decisions.

Righteousness. The Hebrew word for "righteousness" is *tsedeq,* whose root meaning is "straight." Righteousness is that which conforms to the norm, and for the Hebrews that norm is the character of God. Righteousness means, literally, sticking to the straight and narrow, or not going astray. These familiar idioms have the ring of truth. In verses 8 and 9, Wisdom claims that there is nothing "twisted" or "crooked" in her words; they are "all straight to one who understands." It is fascinating that these idioms and adjectives are also applicable to roads. It does not seem to be out of line to say that when we come to the crossroads of our lives, God's wisdom can show us how to determine which way is the "straight way" and which will be twisted or crooked. In the Old Testament, "straightness," or "righteousness," was strongly ethical. It included concepts of justice (equal rights for all), benevolence (showing mercy to the poor), as well as the ethical conduct demanded by the Mosaic law (doing what is right). In the Sermon on the Mount, Jesus gives a definition of righteousness that goes beyond the

Mosaic law, calling for going the second mile and loving one's enemies (Matt. 5:41, 44). True righteousness means "walking the walk," not just "talking the talk." For Paul, righteousness is the gift of God through Christ (Rom. 3:22). God's grace enables us to walk the walk, to choose the straight way.

Jeremiah 6:16: Good Ways

Jeremiah 6:16 is one of the most significant verses in the entire book of Jeremiah. The prophet's message is one of the impending doom of Judah and Jerusalem. The fulfillment of his prophecy was already in progress. Jerusalem had surrendered to the Babylonians in 597 B.C., and this was followed by a second siege, which destroyed the city in 587 B.C. Jeremiah minces no words in explaining the cause of this doom: the people had refused the "ancient paths" and the "good way," saying, "We will not walk in it" (6:16). They had closed their ears to God's word (6:10) and become complacent. They had grown careless about their moral conduct. Jeremiah dared to suggest that there was a connection between their behavior and the doom of the nation.

The road imagery is clear in Jeremiah 6:16. They were at a crossroads. Jeremiah suggests they do four things:

1. Look for the ancient paths. Paths become overgrown when they are not well used, and it may take diligence and concentration to find them. Jesus warned that the "road is easy that leads to destruction, and there are many who take it" but the "road is hard that leads to life, and there are few who find it" (Matt. 7:13–14).
2. Ask for the ancient paths and where the good way lies. Stop and ask directions. This is good advice, and can save a lot of time. There are skilled guides and travel agents who can tell us exactly how to get back on the right path. For, as Marjorie Thompson writes in *Soul Feast*, "Our journeys are not meant to be utterly solitary. Trying to be faithful to God can be a lonely and trying path. We need each other."[17]

3. Walk in the good way. It's not enough to know the path is there. As our friends in Africa say, "Put your feet in the path!" It takes commitment to make the journey. It takes perseverance. It takes determination. In Jeremiah 18:15, the prophet shows what happens when we leave the good way: "My people have forgotten me . . . ; they have stumbled in their ways, in the ancient roads, and have gone into bypaths, not the highway, making their land a horror, a thing to be hissed at forever."

4. Find rest for your souls. I find this metaphor particularly intriguing. Walking is tiring. Our energy runs out. Our leg muscles ache. We know what it means to be "weary travelers." So what does Jeremiah mean, when he says "Walk . . . and find rest"? I believe it has to do with the goal of those ancient paths, that good way. It is very likely that Jesus was thinking of these words when he said, "Come to me, all you that are weary and are carrying heavy burdens, and I will give you rest. Take my yoke upon you, and learn from me; for I am gentle and humble in heart, and you will find rest for your souls" (Matt. 11:28–29). For those who experienced the "ancient paths" as a wearisome burden of legalism, Jesus offers a less burdensome way of following them. The good way is one that follows the double commandment of love, and emphasizes justice, mercy, and faithfulness.

CONCLUSION

Something wonderful happens at crossroads. New opportunities surface; new adventures are possible; new discoveries are made. The whole direction of one's life can change. Values can become clearer; perspectives sharper. The very process of choice making helps us find out something about ourselves. The actor Tom Hanks, in describing how his role as a shipwreck survivor in the movie, *Castaway*, had autobiographical dimensions, said, "There's this concept of being at the crossroads of one's life, and feeling as though that is exactly where you're supposed to be."[18] When we view crossroads as places where we are supposed to be, decision making loses its terror and offers the gift of joyful hope. Jean Blomquist, a woman who was struggling with the crossroads of a painful divorce, wrote: "By calling us beyond what we are or think we can be, whether in relation to ourselves or others, God surprises us with a sense of the potential of our own fuller humanity, our being in the very image of God."[19] As I look back over the times in my life when my road came to one of the "larger ways" Tolkien mentions in the epigram at the beginning of this chapter, I realize that life took on a different shape because of decisions I made at those crossroads: college, marriage, pregnancy, the missionary life, seminary and ordination, retirement. Those decisions led me to places where I was "supposed to be," even though the decision making was not always easy at the time. God surprises us with gifts we do not anticipate at crossroads.

GUIDEPOSTS FOR YOUR JOURNEY

1. As you think about the significant crossroads in your life, reflect on these questions:

   Where was God moving me in this decision?
   Where did God touch me and change me as a result of this decision?
   Where was the challenge difficult?
   What new life did it give me?

2. What does it mean to choose life? to choose death? In a recent newspaper, look for stories of choices made by individuals, groups, or nations for life or for death. If you are in a group, bring clippings to share with the group. Compile lists of choices for life and for death. What are the implications of these lists?

3. Who has shown *hesed* to you as Katherine Sakenfield describes it? To whom have you shown *hesed*?

6   FOLLOWERS OF THE WAY

For my thoughts are not your thoughts,
   nor are your ways my ways.
                     —Isaiah 55:8

I am the way, and the truth, and the life.
                     —John 14:6

In the middle of the journey of our life I came to myself within a dark wood where
the straight way was lost.

                     —Dante Alighieri, *The Divine Comedy*

Which way do I go?

This is a geographical question, a behavioral question, a moral question, and a theological question. It's a question most of us have asked at some point in our lives. It's the critical question at crossroads, because it affects future directions and determines, in part, future choices. In Scripture, it is the ultimate question: the way we answer it is a matter of life and death. Most religions refer to their adherents as pilgrims "on the way" toward some spiritual goal. Taoism, for instance, sees life as a path toward truth. An important understanding of that journey in Taoism is indicated by the expression "wu wei," going with the flow, not pushing or controlling. In Judaism, the Talmud developed as an oral commentary on the Hebrew Bible in order to define more sharply the directions for "walking in the right way." These directions were known as the "halakah," literally, "the going." The way we walk is a clue to who we are and what is important to us.

The word "way" has complex and varied meanings in Scripture. It is a translation of the Hebrew word *derek* (which we discussed in chapter 1) and the Greek word *odos*, and occurs 671 times in the New Revised Standard Version. Although most of these references are literal, geographical references to roads, paths, or journeys, in other places the word "way" refers to patterns of behavior, moral choices, or theological direction. In at least one narrative in Scripture, each of these four different meanings appears. It is the curious story of Balaam, found in Numbers 22–24. Balaam was not an Israelite, but a professional seer, or prophet, from the Mesopotamian valley whose words, it was believed, had the power to curse or bless. Balak, the king of Moab, fearful of the Israelites who were moving into Canaan, wanted to hire Balaam to curse them. It is not Balak who shapes Israel's history, however, but God. God comes to Balaam and tells him to go to Balak, but to do "only what I tell you." Apparently, in his own mind and ignoring God's order, Balaam was wavering between blessing and cursing as he traveled toward Moab, for suddenly an angel of the Lord blocked the narrow path between two vineyard walls. Balaam's donkey had "no way to turn" (behavioral meaning), and the donkey reproached Balaam with the question, "Have I been in the habit of treating you this way?" (moral meaning). The angel, speaking to Balaam for God, explained that Balaam's way is blocked because "your way is perverse before me" (theological meaning). At the end of the story, King Balak of Moab, after trying unsuccessfully to get Balaam to curse Israel, "went his way" (Num. 24:25) (geographical meaning).

The most important of these various meanings of the word "way" is quite obviously the theological one. Many passages in Scripture speak of the way or ways of God or the Lord, referring to God's will. The way of the Lord also means the kind of life that God requires of us. This is described in the Hebrew Bible with terms such as "the good way" (Jer. 6:16); "the right way" (Ps. 50:23); "the way of wisdom" (Prov. 4:11); "the way of righteousness" (Prov. 8:20); and "the way of peace" (Isa. 59:8). The

New Testament sees Jesus as an exemplar of one who walked God's way—"the way, and the truth, and the life" (John 14:6).

All the possible meanings—geographical, behavioral, moral, and theological—contain the image of "taking a road, a path, or a direction." There is always the possibility of a right way or a wrong way. The biblical story is about finding the right way: God's way.

LED ALONG THE WAY: GEOGRAPHICAL PATHS

Following road maps is not always easy, even with the help of computer-generated programs. "Which way should we go?" has been the occasion of many heated discussions between husbands and wives. A few years ago, my spouse and I were taking our little granddaughter Maggie back to Atlanta when such a discussion began. As I subsided into a slightly miffed silence because Dan had chosen not to follow *my* preferred route, I heard a small voice from the back seat: "Grandma, why are you and Grandpa fighting? I didn't think old people would fight!" I'll never forget the chagrin I felt before we burst into laughter. What Dan and I needed was not foolish arguing, but clear and specific guidance from someone wiser to tell us which road to take. This, in a nutshell, is one of the most important lessons in Scripture about journeying.

The fascinating thing is that when Scripture talks about guidance on the way, it refers not only to spiritual guidance, but also to being led along real roads, where we have to make real choices, and where the maps are confusing. Dan and I have traveled many roads; we have been lost in cities and on mountains; we have experienced the weariness of long hours on interstate highways and the heart-stopping moments of roadblocks in Congo's tumultuous days after independence. We experienced the long, fearful road of evacuation from that country when things fell apart, traveling through ten countries in eleven days on our way home. "Which way do we go?" has been a poignant, pain-filled question in our lives.

Because of this, when I read the stories of the geographical movements of God's people in Scripture, from the patriarchs to Paul, I have a sense of identification with them. What kept them going on their journeys? What can we learn from their stories?

The Patriarchs

Geographical movement is dominant in the saga stories of the patriarchs. They traveled from Ur to Haran, to Canaan, to Egypt, and back to Canaan. Interspersed in the accounts of their travels are some revealing uses of the word "way."

First, it is used with the ancient Middle East's traditional code of hospitality. Abraham not only welcomed the three strangers at the entrance of his tent and fed them, but he "went with them to set them on their way." Isaac does the same thing after making a peace treaty with Abimelech, Ahuzzath, and Phicol and feasting with them in Genesis 26:28–31. This act of accompanying strangers a part of the way on their journey was a sign of hospitality, courtesy, and protection. It seems to be echoed in the Twenty-third Psalm, when after the banquet prepared by the Lord, the psalmist exclaims, "Surely goodness and mercy shall follow me all the days of my life." God provides us with blessing and protection, and accompanies us on the way, not just for a part of the journey, but for all of it.

Second, in the patriarchal narratives it is always clear that it is God who leads the way. This is vividly stated in the story of Abraham's quest for a wife for Isaac in Genesis 24. Abraham sent his servant to the city of Nahor near Haran to find a kinswoman for Isaac to marry. The servant's strong faith finds expression in the phrase "The LORD has led me," which he uses to Rebekah at the well (Gen. 24:27) and later repeats to Laban in several variations (Gen. 24:40, 42, 48). This phrase is more than a geographical statement; it is an acknowledgment of unswerving belief in God's steadfast love and faithfulness *(hesed)*. It is worth noting that this idea of being led by God "on the way" is not expressed by any of the patriarchs themselves until after Jacob's Bethel dream of a ladder reaching to heaven. Jacob is not nearly so self-assured as Abraham's servant, and when he makes a vow, he uses a series of "ifs": "*If* God will be with me; *if* God will keep me in this way that I go; *if* God will give me food to eat and clothing to wear; *then* the LORD shall be my God" (Gen. 28:20, 21, italics added). This is the hesitant, bargaining sort of way we often choose for our prayers, not the clear affirmation of faith and trust found in the servant's phrase "The Lord has led me."

The Exodus

The idea of God's actually leading the way does not appear again until the exodus narrative. The storyteller says that when Pharaoh finally relented and let the people go,

> God did not lead them by way of the land of the Philistines, although that was nearer, . . . [but] led the people by the roundabout way of the wilderness toward the Red Sea.
>
> (Exod. 13:17–18)

The Lord used a pillar of cloud by day and a pillar of fire by night "to lead them along the way" (Exod. 13:17–18, 21).

The people's failure to recognize that God is leading them, and to have the same unswerving belief in God's steadfast love and faithfulness as had Abraham's servant, is acknowledged in Moses' farewell address to them, where he reminds them:

> The LORD your God carried you, just as one carries a child, all the way that you traveled until you reached this place. But in spite of this, you have no trust in the LORD your God, who goes before you on the way to seek out a place for you to camp, in fire by night, and in the cloud by day, to show you the route you should take."
>
> (Deut. 1:31–33)

This wonderful passage contains two metaphors for God's leading. In the first, God carries the people as a mother or father carries a child, a way of leading that implies tenderness, solicitude, strength, and loving care. In the second, God leads by going ahead of the people to prepare the campsite and to show them the right road, a way of leading that shows thoughtfulness, providence, and guidance. God eases the path for them. These words find an echo in Jesus' assurance: "If I go and prepare a place for you, I will come again and take you to myself" (John 14:3). When Thomas asked directions, Jesus answered "I am the way. . . ." Moses does not just scold the people; he urges them to

> remember the long way that the LORD your God has led you . . . in order to humble you, testing you to know what was in your heart, whether or not you would keep his commandments.
>
> (Deut. 8:2)

The roads and ways we travel not only provide opportunities for God to demonstrate loving care for us; they provide opportunities for us to learn humility, faithfulness, and obedience.

New Testament

The New Testament uses the word "way" in a geographical, or physical, sense in the accounts of Jesus going up to Jerusalem (Matt. 20:17; Luke 13:22 and 17:11), the disciples' arguments about greatness (Mark 9:33), Jesus and the disciples going to Bethany (Luke 10:38), meeting Bartimaeus (Mark 10:52) and the lepers (Luke 17:11–12), and in Jesus' reference in John 14:4 to "the way to the place where I am going." In fact, so many of the incidents in the Gospels take place during Jesus' various journeys, that it is surprising that the phrase "on the way" does not appear more often. The Gospels are not particularly concerned with geographical data, of course, and only three specific roads are mentioned. The first is the road from Jerusalem to Jericho in the parable of the good Samaritan (Luke 10:31), and the other is the road from Jerusalem to Gaza traveled by Philip in Acts 8:26. The only time the risen Christ is pictured as a traveler is "on the road" to Emmaus (Luke 24:32, 35).

The Greek word *odos,* translated as "way," also occurs in many references to Paul's travels on his missionary journeys, but the references do not cite particular roads, only general descriptions, such as the one in the letter to the Romans, "I will set out by way of you to Spain" (Rom. 15:28), and to the Corinthians, "I wanted to visit you on my way to Macedonia" (2 Cor. 1:16).

THE USE OF PERSONAL PRONOUNS

Frequently the word "way" is used in conjunction with personal pronouns: his way, her way, their way, your way, our way, or my way. Although these expressions appear to be offhand and casual at first glance, they are actually of significance, because they occur during some of the most poignant moments in Scripture:

> After Jacob's peace treaty with Laban at Mizpah, he "went on his way." (Gen. 32:1)
>
> When Naomi urged her daughters-in-law to "turn back, . . . go your way" as she was leaving Moab. (Ruth 1:12)
>
> After Hannah prayed for a son, and received Eli's promise that her prayer would be granted, she "went her way." (1 Sam. 1:18 RSV)
>
> After Samuel denounced Saul, saying, "You have done foolishly; you have not kept the commandment of the LORD your God. . . . Now your kingdom will not continue" (1 Sam. 13:13–14), he "went on his way." (1 Sam. 13:15)
>
> After David spared the sleeping Saul's life, and received Saul's blessing, he "went his way." (1 Sam. 26:25)
>
> When Jesus "made his way" to Jerusalem (Luke 13:22) and announced his intention to face his death by saying, "I must be on my way." (Luke 13:33)
>
> When Jesus forgave the woman accused of adultery, and said "Go your way, and from now on do not sin again." (John 8:11)
>
> When Jesus said to the disciples in the upper room, "Rise, let us be on our way." (John 14:31)

In these passages, "way" refers not to an abstract, impersonal, choiceless superhighway, but to a highly personal, emotionally charged moment in the lives of individuals. "Going my way" is more than just the title of an old movie. After intense moments in our lives—the loss of loved ones (as with Naomi, Ruth, and Orpah), accomplishing difficult acts of forgiveness (as with David), or facing suffering (as with Jesus), we have to "go our way," choosing future directions for our ordinary days.

The liturgical calendar for the church year reflects this: after the high and holy feast days, filled with the intensity of celebrating the birth, death, resurrection, and ascension of the Lord, we return to "ordinary days" which comprise the greater part of the year. We keep on faithfully, going our way, knowing that there will be more intense moments ahead.

A WAY OF LIFE: BEHAVIORAL PATHS

When Dan and I arrived in the Congo, we became vividly aware that we were living among people who had a different way of life. Their food and dress was different; they had different customs for marriages and burials. Their lives were governed by tribal loyalties that were strange to us. Polygamy was not uncommon, nor was consulting the "ngangabuka," or witch doctor. We found ourselves saying frequently, "It's their way of life." When we said this, we were referring to total patterns of behavior, or lifestyles. We also said occasionally about particular acts or decisions of our African friends, "It's their way of doing it." In both Hebrew and Greek, the word "way" covers both situations. It can refer to specific patterns of behavior, as in "the way of an adulteress" (Prov. 30:20), or to behavior in general, "keeping his children submissive and respectful in every way" (1 Tim. 3:4). In most cases, it is morally neutral, not implying right or wrong.

This usage of "way" as it refers to behavior is found in both the Hebrew Bible and the New Testament. Specific instructions in the Hebrew Bible include rules for making a sacrifice, such as, "Offer it in such a way that it is acceptable on your behalf" (Lev. 19:5). In the New Testament, "way" refers to a person's behavior, or typical manner of doing things:

> The scribes critique Jesus' words of forgiveness: "Why does this fellow speak in this way?" (Mark 2:7)

Jesus critiques the scribes and Pharisees: "You have a fine way of rejecting the commandment of God in order to keep your tradition!" (Mark 7:9)

The chief priests and scribes search for "a way to kill him." (Mark 11:18)

The description of Jesus' return: "This Jesus . . . will come in the same way as you saw him go into heaven." (Acts 1:11)

Other general patterns of usage are indicated by phrases such as, in the Hebrew Bible, "Every matter has its time and way" (Eccl. 8:6); and, in the New Testament, Paul's reference to the Athenians as "extremely religious . . . in every way" (Acts 17:22), his promise that the Corinthians would be "enriched in every way" for their generosity (2 Cor. 9:11), his desire not to burden them "in any way" (2 Cor. 11:9), and his defense before Agrippa: "All the Jews know my way of life" (Acts 26:4).

The word "way" is also used idiomatically in expressions such as "the way of women" in Genesis 31:35, a euphemism for menstruation, and "go the way of all the earth" in Joshua 23:14, where it is a euphemism for death. Jeremiah refers to the "way of human beings" being beyond their own control, a reference to God's direction of human life (Jer. 10:23), and there are also references in Scripture to the ways of eagles, snakes, ships (Prov. 30:19), locusts (Joel 2:7), and thunderbolts (Job 28:26).

Behavior is also indicated by a wide assortment of phrases such as "in this way," "in that way," "in such a way," "by whatever way," "in every way," "in the same way," and "in any way." Most memorably, one such phrase is found in the Sermon on the Mount, where Jesus compares his followers to a lamp that gives light to all in the house, and says, "in the same way, let your light shine before others" (Matt. 5:16).

THE GOOD WAY: MORAL PATHS

In contrast to the category of behavior, in which "way" has neither positive nor negative connotations, the moral category makes a clear distinction between the "right way" and the "wrong way," or the "good way" and the "evil way." Although our African friends had different ways of behavior, for example, we were in strong agreement on many important moral issues: that murder, rape, child molestation, and theft were evil ways, and that generosity, hospitality, love of family, care of widows and orphans, and respect for the elderly were good ways.

The story of Potiphar's wife (Gen. 39) contains one of the first uses in Scripture of "way" to describe moral (or immoral) action. Her story sounds much like an early version of a soap opera. Potiphar was one of Pharaoh's officers, and a captain of the guard. He had bought Joseph, who was "handsome and good-looking," from the Ishmaelite slave traders who had taken Joseph to Egypt. Joseph did well in his employ, and Potiphar made him overseer of his house, leaving "all that he had in Joseph's charge." Potiphar's wife, attracted to Joseph, tried to seduce him, but he refused to betray his master or sin against his God. She persisted. He continued to refuse. One day, as he denied her advances she snatched at his linen loincloth, then accused him of attempted rape, and exclaimed to her husband, "This is the way your servant treated me." Here, her use of the word "way" implies a violation of standards of right and wrong.

This recognition of the duality of moral choice implied by "right way" and "wrong way" pervades the Bible, and becomes a choice metaphor for the kind of crossroads decisions discussed in chapter 4. Prophets such as Samuel felt it was their duty to instruct people in "the good and right way," so that they would make correct moral choices. The history of the kings is punctuated by mention of their "evil ways." Jereboam and Asa became prototypes of those making bad moral choices, which Scripture indicates by using phrases such as "walking in the way" of Jereboam or Asa to imply immoral conduct. Eventually this phrase became enlarged to "walked in the way of the kings of Israel, [and] did what was evil." In contrast to these evil kings, Josiah "walked in all the way of his father David; he did not turn aside to the right or to the left" (2 Kings 22:2). In the New Testament, the use of "way" to indicate moral choice continues: Jude describes false teachers as going "the way of Cain" (Jude 11).

Both Psalms and Proverbs are fond of contrasting the "the way of the righteous" with "the way of the wicked." Psalm 1 is a notable example:

> Happy are those
>   who do not follow the advice of the wicked,
> or take the path that sinners tread,
>   or sit in the seat of scoffers;
> but their delight is in the law of the LORD,
>   and on his law they meditate day and night.
> They are like trees
>   planted by streams of water,
> which yield their fruit in its season,
>   and their leaves do not wither.
> In all that they do, they prosper.
>
> The wicked are not so,
>   but are like chaff that the wind drives away.
> Therefore the wicked will not stand in the judgment,
>   nor sinners in the congregation of the righteous;
> for the LORD watches over the way of the righteous,
>   but the way of the wicked will perish.

It is clear that this psalm sees life as following a "way," a road, or a path. A choice has to be made between the "way of the righteous," over which the Lord watches, and the "way of the wicked," which is a fatal trap. The righteous have a guide for the road in the form of "the law of the LORD." The wicked have nothing in the final analysis: no substance, no foundation, no defense. They are no more substantial than chaff blown by the wind.

Warnings to and about the wicked are frequently couched in the language of road choices, especially in Proverbs:

> "Let the wicked forsake their way." (Isa. 55:7)
>
> "Do not enter the path of the wicked, and do not walk in the way of evil-doers." (Prov. 4:14)
>
> "The way of the wicked leads astray." (Prov. 12:26)
>
> "The way of the wicked is an abomination to the LORD." (Prov. 15:9)

Proverbs describes the way of the wicked as "like deep darkness" (Prov. 4:19), as the way that "seems right" but "is the way to death" (Prov. 14:12), as the "way that is not good" (Prov. 16:29 and Isa. 65:2), as the "way of the perverse" (Prov. 22:5), "the way of the lazy" (Prov. 15:19), and as the "way of the faithless" (Prov. 13:15).

In contrast to the way of the wicked, the faithful are urged to choose the right way (Ps. 50:23); the way of faithfulness (Ps. 119:30); the way of the good (Prov. 2:20); the way of wisdom (Prov. 4:11), righteousness (Prov. 8:20), peace (Isa. 59:8), and insight (Prov. 9:6); the way that is blameless (Ps. 119:1), pure (Ps. 119:9), everlasting (Ps. 139:24), and upright (Prov. 13:6).

Moral choice making is a major theme in the prophets, as well. Isaiah's words, "and when you turn to the right or when you turn to the left, your ears shall hear a word behind you, saying, 'This is the way; walk in it'" (Isa. 30:21), are echoed in Psalm 143:8, "Teach me the way I should go," and in Proverbs 2:20, "Walk in the way of the good, and keep to the paths of the just." Isaiah compares the way of the righteous to a road that has been carefully graded and smoothed out by God, impediments removed by grace and providence (Isa. 26:7). Not only does God prepare the road for us, says Isaiah, God also takes us by the hand and leads us in the way we should go (Isa. 48:17). When we obediently accept this guidance, and pray the prayer of Psalm 139:24: "See if there is any wicked way in me, and lead me in the way everlasting," we will be able to make the right choices at the crossroads of our lives.

Psalm 37 holds out to us this astonishing promise:

> Our steps are made firm by the LORD,
>   when he delights in our way;
> though we stumble, we shall not fall headlong,
>   for the LORD holds us by the hand.
>   (vv. 23–24)

THE WAY OF THE LORD: THEOLOGICAL PATHS

In Scripture, there is a very fine line between moral and theological decisions. This is because the biblical understanding of right and wrong, of wickedness and goodness, is based on God's expectations of human behavior, as set forth in God's laws and as revealed by God's Son. Morality gains its force and conviction from the deep and passionate understanding that there is a "way of God," a term that refers not only to God's inscrutable behavior, but to the paths God wants us to follow.

When Dan and I were preparing to go to Africa as missionaries, a friend put a very important question to me: "What," she asked, "do you expect to accomplish?" I knew the right answer, of course: We were going to teach God's way. We would accomplish that in classrooms and churches, through Christian education courses and religious dramas and evangelistic itineration. We had it all figured out. What I came to realize after some years in the field was that the only real way to teach God's way is to live it. If we accomplished anything in our efforts to teach God's way, it was probably done over coffee with students, in the kitchen with household help, at dinner with friends, in the yard with our children. The way of God is not an abstract philosophical subject, but an empowering concept for everyday life that shows us the way to live.

God's Ways Are Not Our Ways

When we begin to reflect on God's ways, it would be well to keep in mind the words of Chinese philosopher Lao-tzu,

The Way that can be described is not the eternal way.[1]

This is similar to what Isaiah expressed in chapter 55:

For my thoughts are not your thoughts,
    nor are your ways my ways, says the LORD.
For as the heavens are higher than the earth,
    so are my ways higher than your ways
    and my thoughts than your thoughts."
                                        (Isa. 55:8–9)

The inscrutability of God is a given. We cannot unravel with our finite minds the mystery of God's purposes, decrees, intents, patterns, and will. The Buddhist term for God means, literally, "not that." God is more than anything we can say about God. The title of theologian William Placher's book *The Domestication of Transcendence* contains a stern warning.[2] We must not try to pat God into a shape and size that we can comprehend and with which we can feel comfortable. Pop religion items such as *God's Little Instruction Book* and billboards with the quote " 'Don't Make Me Come Down There!'—God" are examples of the kind of domestication that reduces God to the ordinary and God's rules to a legal code. God is high and holy and awesome. God's ways and thoughts are not our ways and thoughts. In Isaiah 40:28, as in chapter 55, the prophet is picturing God as creator and lord of history:

> The LORD is the everlasting God,
>   the Creator of the ends of the earth.
> He does not faint or grow weary;
>   his understanding is unsearchable.

By pointing to the "unsearchable" character of God's ways, immeasurably greater than can be imagined, Isaiah gives his readers hope. Even in the midst of our weariness and hopelessness, even when nothing seems to be going right, even when God seems to be disregarding our prayers, all things are possible with God. God's ways are still more effective than ours. God IS great in strength. God IS mighty in power. God DOES give power to the faint and strengthen the powerless. It is because of God's inscrutable ways that we "shall go out in joy, and be led back in peace" (Isa. 55:12).

And yet, Scripture does give us tantalizing clues to the recognition that the way of God is a way to be praised, to be taught, to be shared, and to be followed. Praise of God's way is expressed in David's great song of deliverance after the defeat of Saul:

> This God—his way is perfect;
>   the promise of the LORD proves true;
>   he is a shield for all who take refuge in him.

> For who is God, but the LORD?
>> And who is a rock, except our God?
>>> (2 Sam. 22:31–32; see also
>>>> Ps.18:30–31)

In Psalm 77, there is an echo of this praise, which also ends with a rhetorical question:

> Your way , O God, is holy.
>> What god is so great as our God?
>>> (Ps. 77:13)

Even though the way of God is inscrutable, perfect, and holy, it can still be taught. Proverbs 10:29 hints at this in its praise for the way of the Lord as "a stronghold for the upright, but destruction for evildoers." In this case, the way of the Lord probably refers to the moral teachings of the Torah. Other references are even more explicit. Psalm 86, for example, is almost audacious. It extols God with a phrase recognizing God's transcendence—"You alone are God"—but adds the petition "Teach me your way, O LORD, that I may walk in your truth; give me an undivided heart to revere your name" (Ps. 86:11). Psalm 25 is similar: "Make me to know your ways, O LORD, teach me your paths" (Ps. 25:4). It is firm in its conviction that God is willing to do this:

> Good and upright is the Lord;
>> therefore he instructs sinners in the way.
> He leads the humble in what is right,
>> and teaches the humble his way.
>>> (Ps. 25:8–9)

The paradox of faith is that the goal of our lives is to know God, and to walk in God's ways, all the while acknowledging that we can *never* know God, and that God's ways can *never* be our ways. The beauty of faith is that this is not discouraging, but profoundly encouraging. We believe that God sees what we cannot see, and understands what we do not understand. This enables us to move forward with confidence, believing that "all things work together for good for those who love God, who are called according to his purpose" (Rom. 8:28). The wonder of faith is that although the ways of God will never be completely our ways, God can and does teach us what it means to walk in them. When we experience the joy of that walk, we want to share it with others, so that "your way may be known upon earth" (Ps. 67:2).

Walking in God's Way

It is clear that true praise of the way of God cannot be separated from the desire to follow that way. The "teach me your way" petitions in Psalms 27 and 86 reflect that desire. Jeremiah's description of the unfaithful poor, "They do not know the way of the LORD" (Jer. 5:4), equates that way with the law of God. In a graphic image, he says both the poor and the rich have "broken the yoke," refusing to follow God's way. David's charge to Solomon is clear and specific:

> Be strong, be courageous, and keep the charge of the LORD your God, walking in his ways and keeping his statutes, his commandments, his ordinances, and his testimonies, as it is written in the law of Moses.
>
> (1 Kgs. 2:2b–3a)

Later Solomon echoes this charge in his prayer of dedication, asking God to teach the people "the good way in which they should walk" (1 Kgs. 8:36).

What characterizes God's way? Deuteronomy 10:17–18 offers a clue: God is "not partial and takes no bribe, . . . executes justice for the orphan and the widow, and loves the strangers, providing them food and clothing." The Pharisees refer to this definition in their hypocritical flattery that precedes their attempts to entrap Jesus. Their disciples say to Jesus, "We know that you are sincere, and teach the way of God in accordance with truth, and show deference to no one; for you do not regard people with partiality" (Matt. 22:16).

What does it mean for us to "walk in God's ways"? Deuteronomy 10:12–13 provides an answer to that:

What does the LORD your God require of you? Only to fear the LORD your God, to walk in all his ways, to love him, to serve the LORD your God with all your heart and with all your soul, and to keep the commandments of the LORD your God and his decrees that I am commanding you today, for your own well-being.

According to this text, walking in God's way has three distinct components: loving, serving, and keeping God's commandments. None stands alone; all are necessary if we are to walk the walk. Loving God is meaningless if we do not serve God by serving others with acts of kindness, mercy, and justice and do not keep God's commandments in obedience and humility. These three together spell out "the way of God."

Losing Our Way

We cannot look at the references to the word "way" in Scripture without realizing that many of those references spell out how often we human beings lose our way, either by carelessness, by misdirection, by stubborn willfulness, or, as Proverbs reminds us, by moving too hurriedly (Prov. 19:2). Theologian Douglas John Hall wrote these words in 1987, and they seem even more true of the church today:

> It is not an easy matter to find the right path, to do the right thing for the right reason. It is not easy in the first place even to know what is right. For one thing, we ourselves are only beginners—"on the way" *(in via)*. Our personal lives and our life together as the fellowship are plagued by internal confusions. How often throughout these twenty-odd centuries have good intentions been ruined by glandular and other urges, by mixed-up relations within the congregation, by petty jealousies and insidious talk![3]

The story of losing the way begins at the east of the garden of Eden, where a flaming, turning sword prevented Adam and Eve from "the way to the tree of life" (Gen. 3:24). That way was blocked to the human creatures who had corrupted wisdom for the sake of splendor (see Ezek. 28:17). It was blocked because, in the words of Old Testament scholar Walter Brueggemann, they wanted "masterful discernment of all, without the capacity to suffer and be vulnerable."[4] The way left open to them was the road of suffering and vulnerability that they had hoped to avoid: the path of thorns and thistles, of sweat and toil. This story of a "blocked way" reminds us of the enormity of our loss every time we set ourselves up as mini-gods, wanting knowledge without wisdom and power without vulnerability.

Moses' farewell address in Deuteronomy circles back again and again to the harsh theme of "turning from the way." After the incident of the golden calf, the Lord urges Moses to "go down quickly," because the Israelites "have been quick to turn from the way that I commanded them" (Deut. 9:12). In Deuteronomy 11:26–28, Moses utters a severe warning, which includes both blessing and curse. The blessing is the result of obedience to the commandments. The curse will fall on them if they "turn from the way" commanded by Moses and follow other gods. Moses also speaks harshly of the false prophets who spoke treason to turn the Israelites from "the way in which the LORD your God commanded you to walk" (Deut. 13:5). In the last words of Moses' impassioned valedictory, he sounds weary and pessimistic. He reflects the feelings of many discouraged leaders who sense that their words may be falling on stubbornly deaf ears: "For I know that after my death you will surely act corruptly, turning aside from the way that I have commanded you" (31:29). The book of Deuteronomy does not leave us with this discouragement, however. In Moses' final song, he prays that his teaching will "drop like the rain, . . . like gentle rain on grass, like showers on new growth" (32:2). He follows that with an ascription of praise to the greatness of our God. Moses cannot keep his followers from turning from the way; he can only hope and pray that his teaching will be fruitful and produce the new growth of obedience. The rest is up to God.

Isaiah's well-known confession, "All we like sheep have gone astray; we have all turned to our own way" (Isa. 53:6), reminds us that it is not just the ancient Israelites who have failed to follow God's way. One of the prayers of confession in the *Book of Common Worship* of the Presbyterian Church (U.S.A.) begins: "Almighty and merciful God, we have erred and strayed from your ways like lost sheep. We have followed too much the devices and desires of our own hearts."[5]

We lose the way of God, in spite of having the road map of God's Word. Just having a map is never enough. A map, to be effective, must be studied. Confusing crossroads, decisive forks, twists, and turns all become clear when we understand the map. If we are to be faithful pilgrims along God's highway, we will need to live with God's map in our hands, our minds, and our hearts. That's what the book of Deuteronomy is all about.

FOLLOWERS OF THE WAY

In light of the richness of the metaphor "way" in the Hebrew Bible, it is hardly surprising that after Jesus' death, his disciples' earliest self-designation was "followers of the Way." This preceded the term "Christians." Luke uses this term in the story of Saul's conversion, saying that Saul went to Damascus to hunt down "any who belonged to the Way" (Acts 9:2). In his Gospel, Luke had shown a preference for the image of being on a journey as a metaphor for being a follower of Christ, and describes Jesus as a guide who takes his followers to places they would never have experienced without his leading. Walter Brueggemann comments on the metaphor of journey as a way of speaking about faith in the New Testament:

> The "way" as a metaphor is not precisely characterized, but it is variously the way of Jesus, the way of the cross, the way of suffering, the way to Jerusalem. The term marks Christians as those who live in a way contrasted to every fixed and settled form of life. They pursue a God who finally will be at peace with no human arrangement that falls short of the Kingdom in its practice of justice and freedom. "The way" clearly brought the early church into conflict with all the false ways of self-securing.[6]

JESUS AS THE WAY

"The Way," of course, refers to the "way" of Jesus. Jesus used this metaphor in speaking of himself as "the way, and the truth, and the life" (John 14:6). Jesus is the Way because he is the truth, revealing the true nature of the Father, who is the goal of our journey. He is the life, because life comes through the truth. Those who believe the truth that Jesus is the incarnate revelation of the Father receive the gift of life

(John 5:24), because life comes through truth. Jesus is the Way—the way to the truth, the way to life.[7]

Bookstores abound today with titles that offer help for the spiritual journey or ways to spirituality. Not all of these books reflect the New Testament understanding of the "Way." New Testament scholar Richard B. Hays warns, "The danger in the church today, is that we will slide imperceptibly into a generic, self-indulgent religiosity in which anything that comes to us under the guise of 'religion' will be uncritically embraced."[8] Hays suggests that we test these "ways to spirituality" by Paul's criterion in 1 Corinthians 12:3: those who confess that Jesus is Lord are speaking under the influence of the Holy Spirit; those who deny his lordship are not speaking by the Spirit of God.

THE CHRISTIAN WAY

"Way" is used in the New Testament to express a number of important theological ideas. After describing many wonderful spiritual gifts and roles in the body of Christ, Paul challenges his readers to "a more excellent way" to exercise these gifts and roles. The well-known thirteenth chapter of 1 Corinthians describes this way. As Richard B. Hays has noted, Paul is not saying here that love is a higher and better gift, but rather that "it is a 'way', a manner of life within which all the gifts are to find their proper place."[9] It is a way of reaching the goal.

The letter to the Ephesians uses the term "way" in several fashions. There is the "way of life" God has in mind for us, which finds expression in good works (Eph. 2:10). There is the urgent exhortation "Speaking the truth in love, we must grow up in every way into him who is the head, into Christ" (4:15). There is the contrast between the lives of those Gentiles who have "abandoned themselves to licentiousness, " and "the way you learned Christ" (4:19–20) and between the readers' "former way of life" and the "new self" (4:22, 24).

Hebrews mentions the "new and living way" that Christ opened for us (Heb. 10:20). The writer is speaking here of worship, and the transformation brought to it by Jesus. In the old days, only the high priest entered into the "Holy of Holies," the inner sanctum of the Temple. Now Jesus has opened up, as Tom Long phrases it, "a pilgrim way of grace, a highway leading into the very presence of God."[10]

Second Peter warns against false teachers who betray "the way of truth" (2 Pet. 2:2) and "the way of righteousness" (2 Pet. 2:21). These teachers follow "licentious ways," instead, much like the Gentiles about whom the Ephesians were warned. Their behavior "maligns" the way of truth. This is very similar to Jude 4, where false teachers are portrayed as perverting the grace of our God into licentiousness. This clear distinction between the way of truth and righteousness and licentiousness is a reminder that God makes ethical demands of those who would follow the "way of truth," and that those who ignore these demands will suffer the consequences. This is in keeping with the Hebrew Bible's warnings to choose the way of righteousness and avoid the way of the wicked.

The familiar term "way of salvation" is used only once in Scripture, and that is in the shout of a mentally deranged slave girl who followed Paul and Silas around Philippi. What she said was true—"These men are slaves of the Most High God, who proclaim to you a way of salvation" (Acts 16:17)—but her frenzied behavior annoyed Paul to the extent that he quieted her by an exorcism. How curious that he did not use her words as a springboard to his proclamation of the Way! How fascinating that it was a deranged woman who recognized their mission and their loyalty to "the Most High God" and his Way!

LIGHT FOR THE WAY

In the dark places of our lives, it is often difficult to see the way. Dante Alighieri opens the "Inferno" section of his *Divine Comedy* with the words that appear at the beginning of this chapter:

> In the middle of the journey of our life I came to myself within a dark wood where the straight way was lost.

His image of losing "the straight way" in a "dark wood" has struck a familiar chord with many readers through the years. Our sense of loneliness and even of abandonment is at its strongest in those dark woods. Dante had never heard the phrase "mid-life crisis," and yet he described precisely how many feel "in the middle of the journey of [their] life." Familiar landmarks are obscured, signposts disappear in the gloom, and we falter and stumble as we try to discern the right way for our lives.

I have been there, swallowed up in blackness, trying to find some light. In one of those times, I awoke in the night and these lines of poetry were born out of that blackness:

> Would you read the dark for me,
> Alone beneath a black weight sea?

The image of the trackless sea surely reflects a sense of being lost similar to the "dark wood" of which Dante spoke.

Scripture does not deny the reality of paths lost in darkness. It is a recurring theme in the book of Job. Job speaks of leaders wandering in a "pathless waste," who "grope in the dark without light" (Job 12:24–25). Bildad the Shuhite warns Job of the fate of the wicked whose light is put out (18:5) and who are "thrust from light into darkness" (18:18). Eliphaz promises Job that if he repents, light will shine on his ways (22:28). Job mourns for the days when God watched over him, "when his lamp shone over my head, and by his light I walked through darkness" (29:3).

From Genesis 1:3, when God said "Let there be light," to the promise that "the Lord God will be their light," in Revelation 22:5, God is pictured as Light Giver. The route of the exodus was illuminated by the pillar of fire to "give them light on the way in which they should go" (Neh. 9:12, 19; see Exod. 13:21). The psalms make frequent use of this image of God:

> "It is you who light my lamp; the LORD, my God, lights up my darkness." (Ps. 18:28)

> "The LORD is my light and my salvation; whom shall I fear?" (27:1)

> "In your light we see light." (36:9)

"O send out your light and your truth; let them lead me." (43:3)

"Your word is a lamp to my feet and a light to my path." (119:105)

The Lord is called "light" because it is light that drives darkness away. It is in the light that one can see the way.

Isaiah also liked this metaphor. He used it in his challenge to the people: "O house of Jacob, come, let us walk in the light of the LORD!" (Isa. 2:5). Later, light for the way becomes a powerful image of Messianic hope: "The people who walked in darkness have seen a great light" (Isa. 9:2). Jesus quotes this passage in his sermon in the synagogue at Capernaum (Matt. 4:16), and Zechariah paraphrases it in his song (Luke 1:78–79). The first Servant Song in Isaiah includes a wonderfully comforting picture of God as the one who lights up our dark roads.

> I will lead the blind
>   by a road they do not know,
> by paths they have not known
>   I will guide them.
> I will turn the darkness before them into light,
>   the rough places into level ground.
> (Isa. 42:16)

First John has a similar thought: "God is light and in him there is no darkness at all. If we say that we have fellowship with him while we are walking in darkness, we lie and do not do what is true; but if we walk in the light as he himself is in the light, we have fellowship with one another" (1 John 1:5b–7). This is followed later by a warning: anyone who hates another believer "walks in the darkness, and does not know the way to go, because the darkness has brought on blindness" (1 John 2:11). Our hatred and distrust of others makes us blind, brings darkness into our lives, and causes us to lose the way.

The Gospel of John applies the "Light Giver" image to Jesus in a powerful manner. The prologue states that the Word came into a world of darkness and was "the light of all people" (John 1:4). Jesus himself says, "I am the light of the world.

Whoever follows me will never walk in darkness but will have the light of life" (8:12). Later, Jesus hints at his coming death and urges his followers, "Walk while you have the light, so that the darkness may not overtake you" (12:35).

What are we to make of this? The pattern is clear. God has given us light for our darkest moments. That light is most clearly seen in the life of the one who said, "I am the light of the world." When we find ourselves in a dark wood and are conflicted, doubtful, or depressed, we have a Guide who will turn the darkness before us into light.

At a time when I found myself "overtaken by darkness," I wrote these words. I offer them as light for your path, as a candle for your way:

> In the darkest moments at the crossroads of our lives
> when anxiety and fear cover us with blackness,
> when we cannot see the road ahead
> and are afraid to venture even one step for fear of falling,
>   the light of God breaks in!
> Grace is the unexpected beacon
>   whose brightness gives us hope,
>   and whose radiance empowers us
>   to walk through the shadows into God's light.

CONCLUSION

Douglas John Hall asks a provocative question: "We may be on the way, but where are we going?"[11] He suggests that if we are to be true followers of the Way, we must have our goal clearly in mind. Our goal is to "come to the unity of the faith and of the knowledge of the Son of God, to maturity, to the measure of the full stature of Christ" (Eph. 4:13). Hall says that having this goal for our journey as people of the way *(communion viatorum)* gives us "a vision and vantage point from which we may here and now derive perspective and a sense of direction," so that we no longer have to rely on "our own capacity for the journey, our determination, our optimism."[12]

That "vision and vantage point" are spelled out in the "way" in which God's love was definitively revealed to the world: "God sent his only Son into the world so that we might live through him" (1 John 4:9). This is the goal for followers of the Way: to live through him. This is the goal that defines who we are. This is the "way of salvation" for us. This is the way to life.

GUIDEPOSTS FOR YOUR JOURNEY

1. As a Christian, you have been given a role in teaching others the way of the Lord. Perhaps, as a parent or church leader or friend, you have had times of discouragement about the effectiveness of that teaching. Read Moses' prayer in Deuteronomy 32:2–3. Can you think of ways in which your teaching may have caused new growth? Has your example helped others understand "the way of the Lord"? In what ways do you "ascribe greatness to our God," that is, give God the credit?

2. In what ways, do we "domesticate" the transcendence of God? Does our reading material reflect a folksy familiarity with the creator of the universe? Do our prayers? Does our conversation about what God does or does not do?

3. The next time you are in a large bookstore, look over the titles in the spirituality section. Which ones are not based on the understanding that "Jesus is the way"?

7 THE END OF THE JOURNEY

The Heart's True Home

They confessed that they were strangers and foreigners on the earth, for people who speak in this way make it clear that they are seeking a homeland.
—Hebrews 11:13–14

We are not at home where we live, but where we are loved and understood.
—Old motto

The journey homewards, coming home, that's what it's all about.
—Madeleine L'Engle, 1980

Home is a place where someone is waiting for you.
—Nora Gallagher, 2000

In 1970, after seventeen years of marriage, my husband and I bought the first house we had ever owned. It was in the small village of Willington, South Carolina, where I was born and where we now live. The area was settled by Scots-Irish Presbyterians and French Reformed Huguenots, among whom were my own immigrant ancestors. After making the purchase, I tried to express the deep emotion I felt on finally having a home of our own after years of being on the road.

Now I am home again
>   beneath the pine tree blows
>   and sweet hot purpling of wisteria.
The slow bend road remembering
>   ascends into familiar forest cool
>   and zippers up the long scratched cotton fields.
I stand at last upon the sloping bank
>   where, hesitant, my father's fathers came
>   to seek (oh, God, a haven did they say?)
>   and found instead despair and death . . .
>   but persevered, and planted seed, created home.
So, I, two hundred years behind,
>   have crossed my private sea
>   and choose this known, so peaceful countryside
>   to be my haven, too,
>   where I may plant my seeds and persevere.

We now live in that village. We have come home. The very act of leaving the long and winding road that we have traveled for forty years has caused me to reflect, not only on the meaning of roads, but on the meaning of the destination at the end of those roads: home. Why does coming home feel so good? Why is there such a deep satisfaction at the end of our journeys when we turn into familiar driveways, or see familiar faces smiling in welcome? Journeys can be alluring, the gypsy urge powerful, but Madeleine L'Engle was right when she said, "The journey homewards, coming home, that's what it's all about."[1]

That is what the one story of the Bible is all about, too. The homesickness that began east of Eden, with the exile of Adam and Eve, continued through the sojourning of the patriarchs, the wandering in the wilderness, and the exile in Babylon. Over and over again, the prophets returned to the theme of "homesickness." This theme was expressed both in promises that God would bring the exiles home, and in urgent pleas for God's people to return home in a spiritual sense with renewed obedience, loyalty, and commitment. As we saw in chapter 3, the verb *shub* means to turn around, to return, and to have fortunes restored. All of these are images of "going home" in the deepest and fullest sense. Some of the most cherished assurances in the psalms are that God gives the desolate a home to live in (Ps. 68:6), and that our true home or "dwelling place" is with God (Ps. 90:1).

In the New Testament, we find the people's longing for home expressed in the pilgrimage feasts to "God's home," the temple, and in their longing for a restored nation, where they can truly be "at home" without foreign intruders. Jesus spoke of going home to his Father's house, where there are many "dwelling places," and where he will make ready one of those dwelling places, or homes, for us (John 14:2). The letter to the Ephesians addresses their homesickness by reminding them that they are "no longer strangers" but "members of the household of God" (Eph. 2:19). In common parlance, that means: Take your shoes off; you've come home. The answer to our deepest longings for home is found in the glorious imagery of the twenty-first chapter of Revelation, which raises the fascinating question: Do we ultimately go home to God, or does God come home to us?

One thing is clear: We are doomed to be perpetual wanderers, weary of feet and spirit, until we find home.

WHAT IS HOME?

If we say that the goal of our journeying is to be at home, we must be clear about what we mean by the word "home." Home has been defined in many ways in popular culture and literature. It's where you hang your hat, where the heart is, where someone is waiting for you. I once heard humorist Garrison Keillor say on his radio show, "Home is the place, when you get there, you know where you are." Almost everyone is familiar with Robert Frost's interpretation of home as the place where "when you have to go there they have to take you in." The best definition I've found, however, is the one given me by Trent Moore, a sixteen-year-old member of my congregation: "Home is where you belong."

Even if we leave home for a joyful adventure or in a spirit of rebellion, there will probably come a moment on a lonely road or in a foreign land when a longing for "home" sweeps over us. Paul addresses that longing in his letter to the Romans:

> For no one of us lives, and equally no one of us dies, for himself alone. If we live, we live for the Lord; and if we die, we die for the Lord. Whether therefore we live or die, we belong to the Lord.
>
> (Rom. 14:7–8 NEB)

The Heidelberg Catechism puts the question boldly: "What is your only comfort, in life and in death?" The answer given is "That I belong—body and soul, in life and in death—not to myself but to my faithful Savior, Jesus Christ."[2]

Home is the answer to the restlessness that thrusts us into mobility, to the darkness of the lonely road, to the agony of decisions at crossroads. "The way" about which Jesus spoke is the way home. Being followers of the Way means that we know where home is and we are on our way there. Home is where we belong. We belong to God. Therefore, God is our heart's true home. This simple syllogism contains profound truth. The goal of our journeying is to be at home, to be with God, to be made whole and complete.

THE ROAD HOME

In the late 1960s, a philosophy teacher named Jean Vanier began a remarkable journey. He created a home for people with mental handicaps in a village near Paris. He has reflected on that experience in his deeply moving book *Our Journey Home*. He gave that title to his book because he believes that "home is where we are safe. . . . 'Going home' is a journey to the heart of who we are, a place where we can be ourselves and welcome the reality of our beauty and our pain. From this acceptance of ourselves, we can accept others as they are and we can see our common humanity."[3] Jean Vanier has given his life to creating a home for others who needed a place of belonging, and in the process has found where he belongs.

What Vanier has described as "going home" is capsuled in the Greek word *teleios,* which can be translated as "mature," "complete," "whole," "perfect," "fulfilled," "undivided," or "accomplishing a goal." In other words, *teleios* describes those who have come home: they have reached the goal toward which they have been moving. They are totally at home with God, undivided in obedience and abiding in love. "Whoever lives in love lives in union with God and God lives in union with him" (1 John 4:16b TEV).

When we feel truly at home, it shows. We are at ease, we can be ourselves, we can untie our ties and wear comfortable clothing. When we are at home with God, it also shows. We forgive. We make peace. We love our enemies. We do this because "we know that we belong to God" (1 John 5:19 TEV).

Glimpses of Home

"Are we there yet?" Anyone who has been in a car with small children is familiar with this question. And the honest answer to the theological question about our going home is, "Not yet." At least "not yet" in the sense of being completely and totally at home, undivided in obedience and constantly abiding in love. And yet, in a real sense, the journey itself *is* home. We are not alone in our pilgrimage. Our God goes with us. "The eternal God is your dwelling place, and underneath are the everlasting arms" (Deut. 33:27 RSV). We are "at home" while moving toward "home." This paradox runs through Scripture from beginning to end. We may feel like strangers and exiles on the earth, pilgrims and outsiders, but we have already had a taste, a glimpse, of home. The promise of home in the fullest sense keeps sounding in our ears as we journey.

Two contemporary religious writers have written of this journey and those glimpses in moving language of the heart. The first is a Presbyterian minister, Frederic Buechner. In his book *Longing for Home* he speaks of having glimpses of our heart's true home in "the charity and justice and order and peace" of homes he has known. Then he adds,

> I cannot claim that I have found the home I long for every day of my life, not by a long shot, but I believe that in my heart I have found, and maybe have always known, the way that leads to it. I believe that the home we long for and belong to is finally where Christ is. I believe that home is Christ's kingdom, which exists both within us and among us as we wend our prodigal ways through the world in search of it.[4]

The second is the late C. S. Lewis, an Anglican layman and well-known Christian apologist. Like Buechner, he believed that many of our experiences of Christ's kingdom on earth give us glimpses of what heaven might be like:

> All the things that have ever deeply possessed your soul have been but hints of it—tantalizing glimpses, promises never quite fulfilled, echoes that died away just as they caught your ear. But if it should really become manifest—if there ever came an echo that did not die away but swelled into the sound itself—you would know it. Beyond all possibility of doubt you would say "Here at last is the thing I was made for."[5]

Lewis makes the same point in his children's book *The Last Battle*, when the central characters arrive in the new Narnia (heaven) and recognize it as their "real country," the land for which they had been looking all their lives.[6]

Both of these writers are struggling with a powerful truth, one Jesus tried to communicate to his followers through the kingdom parables. The truth is couched in a paradox: the kingdom is here and now, and the kingdom is not yet. Heaven lies around us, and heaven is our ultimate goal. We see quick flashes of the kingdom of heaven, like glimpses of sunshine through the slats of a blind, but its completeness is still a hidden mystery. It is present in our deep longings, in our deep loves, in moments of beauty, tenderness, and grace. I have experienced these glimpses in the luminous smile of a grandchild running to meet me, in the radiant beauty of a Chinese woman singing "Jesus, the Bright Morning Star," in the prayers of the worshiping community of Taizé in France, and while digging sweet potatoes with the Koinonia Partners of South Georgia. These glimpses both sustain me in my journey and give me assurance about that which is to come—my final destination, my home.

HOMECOMING

The biblical story is not just about the road; it is also about the homecoming that lies at the end of the road. There is a looking-forwardness in Scripture to which we give the solemn name "eschatology." The American Bible Society published a

New Testament for truckers and gave it the title *The Road Home*. They capitalized on the truth that it is the promise of home that keeps truckers going. It is that promise that is clear in Jeremiah's prophecy:

> For surely I know the plans I have for you, says the LORD, plans for your welfare and not for harm, to give you a future with hope. . . . I will restore your fortunes and gather you from all the nations and all the places where I have driven you, says the LORD, and I will bring you back to the place from which I sent you into exile.
>
> (Jer. 29:11, 14b)

The book of Jeremiah uses four verbs to describe this homecoming vividly—gather, love, heal, and forgive. A closer look at these verbs will give us a better understanding of the beautiful promises held out by a loving God as we journey toward our heart's true home.

Gather

A homecoming is a gathering together of scattered family members. In Jeremiah 31:8, God promises:

> I am going to bring them from the land of the north,
>   and gather them from the farthest parts of the earth,
> . . . together;
> a great company, they shall return here.

A similar promise is made by God in Zephaniah, which connects the "gathering" even more explicitly with the idea of home:

> I will bring you home,
> at the time when I gather you.
>   (Zeph. 3:20)

A few years ago at Thanksgiving, my grandfather's descendants gathered in the village where he had lived, to celebrate the first family reunion in fifty years.

My ninety-seven-year-old Aunt Robbie flew from California with her daughters for the occasion. Cousins met each other for the first time. We marveled over little ones we had never seen. We gathered in the community center building that had been the school for the older generation. What memories it held for them! At the feast, we laughed together as older family members shared reminiscences, and asked of younger ones, "Now, whose daughter [whose son] are you?" The day would not have been complete without a ritual visit to the two cemeteries where parents and grandparents and great-grandparents lay. This is the kind of joyful reunion the prophets were promising those grieving exiles, and, in the laughter, the hugs, the feast, the celebration, the sense of union with departed loved ones, I caught a glimpse, a foretaste, of the gathering home God has in store for all of us.

Love

The knowledge of God's everlasting, faithful, steadfast love undergirds our homecoming. In Jeremiah 31:3, God promises:

> I have loved you with an everlasting love;
>   therefore I have continued my faithfulness to you.

No clearer picture of that love has ever been drawn than the parable that is not so much about a prodigal son as it is about a forgiving father who was filled with compassion when he saw his son coming home. Our homecoming will be defined and structured by that compassion, not by our "worthiness." We are loved, unconditionally. In commenting on this parable, Henri Nouwen writes about how hard it is for us to really believe this truth.

> Although claiming my true identity as a child of God, I still live as though the God to whom I am returning demands an explanation. I still think about his love as conditional and about home as a place I am not yet fully sure of. While walking home, I keep entertaining doubts about whether I will be truly welcome when I get there. As I look at my spiritual journey, my long and fatiguing trip home, I see how

full it is of guilt about the past and worries about the future. I realize my failures and know that I have lost the dignity of my sonship, but I am not yet able to fully believe that where my failings are great, "grace is always greater."... Belief in total, absolute forgiveness does not come readily.[7]

In spite of our unbelief, however, God continues to love us with an everlasting love, and stands with outstretched arms to receive us home.

Heal

God's promises continue in Jeremiah 30:17:

For I will restore health to you,
   and your wounds I will heal.

Writer Susan Ross defines home as the place "where folks know your name and touch you with love, and give you space to be yourself and you are healed."[8] The places we live often do not provide this kind of touching and healing, and instead are places of wounding. A college student said to me, "I never heard my father say, 'I love you,' as I was growing up. It hurts even now." The wounding is often physical, as well. Surveys show that every twenty-four hours in America, almost 8,500 children or youth are reported abused or neglected.[9] When homes do not supply the health and healing we need, it is important to turn to other sources for help: therapy, support groups, loyal friends, and the church. These places become surrogate homes, and it is there that we can find glimpses of our heavenly home, the home that will not fail us, but will restore us and heal our wounds. The promise of health and healing is a part of John's picture of the New Jerusalem, where "death will be no more; mourning and crying and pain will be no more" (Rev. 21:4).

Forgive

Finally, God makes this wonderful promise in Jeremiah 31:34:

I will forgive their iniquity, and remember their sin no more.

Where God is, love is. Where love is, forgiveness is. The parable of the forgiving father is Jesus' picture of that forgiveness. It is important to remember that this parable in Luke follows on the heels of Jesus' inclusive banquet parables and the Pharisees' grumbling words about Jesus' welcoming acceptance of tax collectors and sinners (Luke 15:1–2). In their complaint, the Pharisees were showing respect for the socially acceptable "who's in and who's out" rules about extending invitations. In the minds of the Pharisees, those rules applied not only to everyday meals, but also to the grand homecoming gathering at the messianic banquet.

Jesus' parable about inviting the riffraff from the streets to a banquet and his act of sitting at table with sinners were loaded with symbolism. Breaking bread was a sign of bonding, of full acceptance, of becoming like family. The parable of the lost son underscores God's embracing and forgiving love. Its message provides a glimpse of what our homecoming will be like. The arms of a welcoming parent will be wrapped around us, and we will know that we belong. We will be forgiven, no matter how many wrong roads we have taken.

The homecoming promise is spelled out boldly in Isaiah 25:6–10. It is the promise of a homecoming feast on Mount Zion, where God will gather all people; where God will heal all people by removing their shrouds of mourning; where God will show love for all people by wiping away the tears from all faces; and where God will forgive the people and take away their disgrace.

A HEAVENLY HOME

There's a lot of confusion in the minds of most of us about that promised home, that better country, that heavenly homeland where the final homecoming gathering will take place. A cover of *Time* magazine showed a man standing on a cloud, shading his eyes as he looks up into the sky, asking, "Does heaven exist?"

We try to assure ourselves by talk about golden streets, pearly gates, and ourselves as angels with wings and harps. We speak of loved ones being "up there" looking down on us. We are even a little apprehensive, especially those of us who are not musical, at the prospect of spending an eternity playing a harp. For some years, I have collected cartoons about heaven (mostly from the *New Yorker*). The picture of heaven in these bits of satire is not always complimentary: it's a "gated" community, which the "marketing guys" have renamed "Birth, Death, and Beyond." Prospective residents are sternly scrutinized by a bearded, winged, haloed St. Peter, who sometimes can't find their names in his computer.

But, actually, Scripture never says that St. Peter is now an angel, equipped with wings and a halo, nor does it promise that we will be. Scripture portrays angels as a different order of beings entirely. Psalm 8 reminds us we are created a "little lower than the angels" (NRSV, margin).

Then what does Scripture say about heaven? Perhaps the best-known description is found in Revelation 21:1–4, which describes a creation that has been transformed into "a new heaven and a new earth." John has a vision of "the holy city, the new Jerusalem, coming down out of heaven from God, prepared as a bride adorned for her husband." Then he hears a voice declaring:

> See, the home of God is among mortals.
> He will dwell with them . . . ;
> they will be his peoples,
> and God himself will be with them;
> he will wipe every tear from their eyes.
> Death will be no more;
> mourning and crying and pain will be no more,
> for the first things have passed away.
> (Rev. 21:3b–4)

John's description of the Holy City continues in 21:21 with details about its jeweled walls and gates and streets of gold. In these passages, he is drawing on word pictures from the apocalyptic traditions of Judaism, which would have been familiar to his readers: the descent of the Holy City to earth on the last day (see Isa. 2:1ff.); the gold and jeweled walls (see Ezek. 28:13); the streets of gold and gates of pearl (cf. Tobit 13:16). John is not writing as a journalist, reporting what he actually saw; he is writing as a poet. He is not trying to answer all questions about the future; he is trying to point to truths that shape lives in the present. John believes that at the end "we meet not an event but a person. . . . God does not merely bring the End, God *is* the End."[10]

Psalm 90 begins with the affirmation: "O Lord, you have always been our home" (v. 1 TEV; "dwelling place" NRSV). This is also what John is affirming when he says, "The home of God is among mortals." Our true home is the place where we know, beyond the shadow of a doubt, that nothing will ever separate us from God's love, where God is as real as our next-door neighbor. Our true home is being with God: the goal of our longing, the end of our heart's journey. All the poetic language about that city, about pearly gates and golden streets, is an attempt to convey the wonder, beauty, and mystery of that oneness with God. Mother Teresa understood this. She said, "Death is nothing but a continuation of life, the completion of life. . . . This life is not the end; people who believe it is, fear death. If it was properly explained that death was nothing but going home to God, then there would be no fear."[11]

Shirley Guthrie answers the question "What then is *heaven*?" with these words: "Not a place located somewhere in outer space where we will escape from our humanity to become angels or disembodied spirits. Heaven is an eternal life of genuine, completely free realization of our humanity in a new heaven and a new earth."[12] Hebrews speaks of entering "God's rest," and this has given rise to the rather dismal images of an eternity of doing nothing except singing hymns. For those of us who like being busy and active, this sounds more like hell than heaven. That's not what God's rest is all about. Entering into God's rest means that, finally, we will be able to be what God wants us to be. It means, Guthrie says, "rest from all the frustration, conflict, and self-contradiction that result from our self-destructive attempts to live without or against God and other people. It means coming to rest or peace with our true selves as we live in free and open community with them."[13] This image is not static or boring. Instead, it is dynamic and active. Life ruled by love is always active. This proper understanding of "eternal rest" paradoxically includes eternal activity and eternal service. In other words, when this provisional existence is over and God brings us home, life really begins.

CONCLUSION

The heart's true home is the culmination of all our hopes and dreams and long-ings, the place where we are gathered, loved, healed, and forgiven, where tears are gone, crying is gone, pain is gone, and everything is new. The moments in this life when Christ's kingdom becomes a reality in us and in others give us a glimpse of what it will be like when we are finally home for good, when we will sit at a home-coming banquet of which the Communion table is a foretaste, when all the weary, faithful pilgrims will sit down in peace, home at last where we belong, where God is—the one who is, indeed, our heart's true home—where, in the words of Julian of Norwich, "All will be well, and all shall be well, and all manner of things will be well."

GUIDEPOSTS FOR YOUR JOURNEY

1. Close your eyes and think about the word "home." What pictures come to your mind? What places? What persons?
2. Read Psalm 137. When have you felt in exile? How did you keep memories of home alive?
3. Write five words that describe home to you. Put some of these words in a one-line definition of home.
4. Which of those five words also describes your understanding of heaven?

NOTES

CHAPTER 1: ROADS IN BIBLICAL TIMES

1. David Dorsey, *The Roads and Highways of Ancient Israel* (Baltimore: Johns Hopkins University Press, 1991), xvii.
2. Ibid., 3.
3. W. S. McCullough, "Ass," in *Interpreter's Bible Dictionary,* vol. 1 (Nashville: Abingdon Press, 1962), 260–61.
4. J. A. Thompson, "Horse," in *Interpreter's Bible Dictionary,* vol. 2 (Nashville: Abingdon Press, 1962), 647.
5. Isaac Mendelsohn, "Travel and Communication in the Old Testament," in *Interpreter's Bible Dictionary,* vol. 4 (Nashville: Abingdon Press, 1962), 689.
6. G. S. Cansdale, "Animals of the Bible," in *The Illustrated Bible Dictionary,* vol. 1 (Wheaton, Ill.: Tyndale House Publishers, 1980), 53.
7. Dorsey, 57.
8. Ibid., 213.
9. Ibid., 223.

CHAPTER 2: THE JOURNEY BEGINS: LEAVING HOME

1. See J. R. R. Tolkien, "The Old Walking Song," in *The Lord of the Rings,* Part 1, *The Fellowship of the Ring* (New York: Ballantine Books, 1965), 62.
2. Norman Gottwald, *The Hebrew Bible: A Socio-Literary Introduction* (Philadelphia: Fortress Press, 1985), 155.
3. Robert Raines, *Going Home* (San Francisco: Harper & Row, 1979), 27.

4. Walter Brueggemann, *Genesis,* Interpretation: A Bible Commentary for Teaching and Preaching (Atlanta: John Knox Press, 1982), 118.

5. Robert Van de Weyer, *Celtic Prayers* (Nashville: Abingdon Press, 1997), 25. Used by permission.

6. James Fowler, *Stages of Faith: The Psychology of Human Development and the Quest for Meaning* (New York: Harper & Row, 1981), 178.

7. Marjorie Thompson, *Soul Feast* (Louisville, Ky.: Westminster John Knox Press, 1995), 104.

8. Suzanne Rahn, *The Wizard of Oz: Shaping an Imaginary World,* Twayne's Masterwork Studies, no. 167 (New York: Twayne Publishers, 1998), 57.

9. Walter Brueggemann, *Cadences of Home: Preaching among Exiles* (Louisville, Ky.: Westminster John Knox Press, 1997), 2.

10. Fred Craddock, *Luke,* Interpretation: A Bible Commentary for Teaching and Preaching (Louisville, Ky.: John Knox Press, 1990), 142.

11. Sara Covin Juengst, "Flight," in *Images: Women in Transition,* ed. Janice Grana (Nashville: The Upper Room, 1976), 134. Used by permission of the publisher.

12. Henri Nouwen, *The Return of the Prodigal Son* (New York: Doubleday, 1992), 32.

13. Douglas John Hall, *When You Pray* (Valley Forge, Pa: Judson Press, 1987), 98.

14. Juengst, "Flight." Used by permission.

CHAPTER 3: ON THE ROAD AGAIN: COPING WITH CHANGE

1. Joshua Cooper Ramo Chama, "Finding God on the Net," *Time,* December 16, 1996, 67.

2. Peter L. Benson and Carolyn H. Eklin, *Effective Christian Education: A National Study of Protestant Congregations* (Minneapolis: Search Institute, 1990), 35.

3. Gerald Celente, quoted in "Angst Breeds Spiritual Searching," by Bill Hendrick, *Atlanta Journal-Constitution,* December 3, 1994, E–1.

4. Gustav Spohn, "Half of American Public Abandon Family's Religion," *The Presbyterian Outlook,* September 12, 1994, 3.

5. Harry Thomas Frank, *Discovering the Biblical World* (New York: Hammond, 1975), 33.

6. Norman K. Gottwald, *The Hebrew Bible: A Socio-Literary Introduction* (Philadelphia: Fortress Press, 1985), 172.

7. John White and James Fadiman, eds., *Relax: How You Can Feel Better, Reduce Stress and Overcome Tension* (The Confucian Press, 1976), 37.

8. Walter Brueggemann, *Hope within History* (Atlanta: John Knox Press, 1987), 23.

9. *Enfolded in Love: Daily Readings with Julian of Norwich* (Minneapolis: Seabury Press, 1981), 55.

10. Thomas Merton, *No Man Is an Island* (Garden City, N.Y.: Image Books, 1955), 75.

11. J. Behm, "Metanoia," in *The Theological Dictionary of the New Testament,* ed. Gerhard Kittel, vol. 4 (Grand Rapids: Wm. B. Eerdmans Publishing Co., 1967), 1002.

12. M. Eugene Boring, *Revelation,* Interpretation: A Bible Commentary for Teaching and Preaching (Louisville, Ky.: John Knox Press, 1989), 214.

CHAPTER 4: THE LONELY ROAD

1. James Weldon Johnson, "The Creation," in *The Questing Spirit,* ed. Halford Luccock (New York: Coward-McCann, 1947), 341.

2. For further information on Semitic hospitality, see Sara Covin Juengst, *Breaking Bread* (Louisville, Ky.: Westminster/John Knox Press, 1992), 39.

3. Stanley Hauerwas and William H. Willimon, *Resident Aliens* (Nashville: Abingdon Press, 1989), 49.

4. Ibid., 12.

5. Ibid., 12–13.

6. Ibid., 39.

7. Walter Brueggemann, *Deep Memory, Exuberant Hope* (Minneapolis: Fortress Press, 2000), 17.

8. Walter Brueggemann, *The Land* (Philadelphia: Fortress Press, 1977), 8.

9. Ibid., 29.

10. Rene Jahiel, *Homelessness: A Prevention Oriented Approach* (Baltimore: Johns Hopkins Press, 1992), 7.

11. Jean Kim, *End Homelessness* (Louisville, Ky.: Presbyterian Hunger Program, Presbyterian Church [U.S.A.], 2000), 18.

12. James L. Mays, *Psalms,* Interpretation: A Bible Commentary for Teaching and Preaching (Louisville, Ky.: John Knox Press, 1994), 347.

13. Douglas R. A. Hare, *Matthew,* Interpretation: A Bible Commentary for Teaching and Preaching (Louisville, Ky.: John Knox Press, 1993), 323.

14. Ann Weems, *Psalms of Lament* (Louisville, Ky.: Westminster John Knox Press, 1995), 30. Used by permission of Westminster John Knox Press.

CHAPTER 5: AT THE CROSSROADS

1. Walter Brueggemann, *Genesis,* Interpretation: A Bible Commentary for Teaching and Preaching (Atlanta: John Knox Press, 1982), 113.

2. Thomas G. Long, *Hebrews,* Interpretation: A Bible Commentary for Teaching and Preaching. (Louisville, Ky.: John Knox Press, 1997), 118.

3. Patrick D. Miller, *Deuteronomy,* Interpretation: A Bible Commentary for Teaching and Preaching (Louisville, Ky.: John Knox Press, 1990), 3.

4. Ibid., 213.

5. Ibid., 214–215.

6. Katherine Doob Sakenfeld, *Ruth,* Interpretation: A Bible Commentary for Teaching and Preaching (Louisville, Ky.: John Knox Press, 1999), 11–12.

7. Ibid., 12.

8. Ibid., 24.

9. Ibid., 33.

10. Ibid., 82.

11. Fred B. Craddock, *Luke,* Interpretation: A Bible Commentary for Teaching and Preaching (Louisville. Ky.: John Knox Press, 1990), 141.

12. Ibid., 144.

13. G. B. Caird, *Saint Luke* (NewYork: Penguin Books, 1963), 205.

14. Mother Teresa of Calcutta and Brother Roger of Taizé, *Meditations on the Way of the Cross* (New York: Pilgrim Press, 1987), 20.

15. Leo G. Perdue, *Proverbs,* Interpretation: A Bible Commentary for Teaching and Preaching (Louisville, Ky.: John Knox Press, 2000), 81.

16. Ibid., 4.

17. Marjorie Thompson, *Soul Feast* (Louisville, Ky.: Westminster John Knox Press, 1995), 116–117.

18. Fred Kaplan, "Gifted and Talented,"in *Entertainment Spotlight, a Publication of The Index-Journal,* July 17, 2000, S-1.

19. Jean Blomquist, "Daily Dancing with the Holy One," *Weavings,* vol. 4, no. 6, November–December 1989, 10.

CHAPTER 6: FOLLOWERS OF THE WAY

1. Alan Watts, "Tao," in *Sources,* ed. Theodore Roszak, Harper Colophon Books (New York: Harper & Row, 1972), 523.

2. See William Placher, *The Domestication of Transcendence: How Modern Thinking about God Went Wrong* (Louisville, Ky.: Westminster John Knox Press, 1996).

3. Douglas John Hall, *When You Pray: Thinking Your Way into God's World* (Valley Forge: Judson Press, 1987), 53.

4. Walter Brueggemann, *Genesis,* Interpretation: A Bible Commentary for Teaching and Preaching (Atlanta: John Knox Press, 1982), 54.

5. *Book of Common Worship* (Louisville, Ky.: Westminster/John Knox Press, 1993), 87.

6. Brueggemann, *Genesis,* 122.

7. Raymond E. Brown, trans., *The Gospel According to John XIII–XXI,* The Anchor Bible, vol. 29 (Garden City, N.Y.: Doubleday & Co., 1970), 630–31.

8. Richard B. Hays, *First Corinthians,* Interpretation: A Bible Commentary for Teaching and Preaching (Louisville, Ky.: John Knox Press, 1997), 222.

9. Ibid., 222.

10. Thomas G. Long, *Hebrews,* Interpretation: A Bible Commentary for Teaching and Preaching (Louisville, Ky.: John Knox Press, 1997), 104.

11. Hall, *When You Pray,* 55.

12. Ibid., 56.

CHAPTER 7: THE END OF THE JOURNEY: THE HEART'S TRUE HOME

1. Madeleine L'Engle, *Walking on Water: Reflections on Faith and Art* (New York: Bantam Books, 1980), 162.

2. *The Constitution of the Presbyterian Church (U.S.A.),* Part I, *Book of Confessions* (Louisville, Ky.: Office of the General Assembly, Presbyterian Church [U.S.A.], 1999), 4.001.

3. Jean Vanier, *Our Journey Home* (Maryknoll, N.Y.: Novalis/Orbis, 1997), xi.

4. Frederic Buechner, *Longing for Home* (San Francisco: HarperSanFrancisco, 1996), 28.

5. C. S. Lewis, *The Problem of Pain* (Glasgow: William Collins Sons & Co., 1949), 116–17.

6. C. S. Lewis, *The Last Battle* (London: Bodley Head, 1956), 172.

7. Henri Nouwen, *The Return of the Prodigal Son* (New York: Doubleday, 1992), 47.

8. Susan Ross, "The Place Where We Are Healed," *Alive Now,* May/June 1989, 13.

9. Quoted in information distributed by Presbyterian Church (U.S.A.) Year of the Child, 2000.

Notes

10. M. Eugene Boring, *Revelation,* Interpretation: A Bible Commentary for Teaching and Preaching (Louisville, Ky.: John Knox Press, 1989), 215.

11. Mother Teresa of Calcutta and Brother Roger of Taizé, *Meditations on the Way of the Cross* (New York: Pilgrim Press, 1987), 49.

12. Shirley Guthrie, *Christian Doctrine,* rev. ed. (Louisville, Ky.: Westminster John Knox Press, 1994), 395.

13. Ibid., 396.

INDEX OF SCRIPTURE REFERENCES

Index of Scripture References